2nd edition

THE PRACTICE OF PHILOSOPHY

A Handbook for Beginners

JAY F. ROSENBERG

*University of North Carolina
at Chapel Hill*

PRENTICE-HALL, INC., *ENGLEWOOD CLIFFS, NEW JERSEY 07632*

Library of Congress Cataloging in Publication Data

ROSENBERG, JAY F. (DATE)
 The practice of philosophy.

 Includes bibliographical references and index.
 1. Philosophy—Introductions. I. Title.
BD21.R644 1984   100   83-9710
ISBN 0-13-687467-3

Editorial/production supervision and
 interior design: Barbara Alexander
Cover design: Wanda Lubelska
Manufacturing buyer: Harry P. Baisley

Printed in the United States of America

10 9 8 7 6 5 4 3 2 1

ISBN 0-13-687467-3

PRENTICE-HALL INTERNATIONAL, INC., *London*
PRENTICE-HALL OF AUSTRALIA PTY. LIMITED, *Sydney*
EDITORA PRENTICE-HALL DO BRASIL, LTDA., *Rio de Janeiro*
PRENTICE-HALL CANADA INC., *Toronto*
PRENTICE-HALL OF INDIA PRIVATE LIMITED, *New Delhi*
PRENTICE-HALL OF JAPAN, INC., *Tokyo*
PRENTICE-HALL OF SOUTHEAST ASIA PTE. LTD., *Singapore*
WHITEHALL BOOKS LIMITED, *Wellington, New Zealand*

In a few years she's going to ask me, "Daddy, just what is it that philosophers do anyway?" Well, that's a long story. Fortunately she can read.
This one is for my daughter, Leslie Johanna.

The crux of a philosophical argument often appears to be a Dedekind cut between a series of 'as I will show's and a series of 'as I have shown's. In a sense the preliminaries *are* the argument, and there is no crux apart from their perspicuous deployment. A few more introductory remarks, therefore, and my job will be done.

—WILFRID SELLARS
Science and Metaphysics

CONTENTS

PREFACE

From time to time a teacher orders a text for some class and, after a semester of frustration, he says to himself, "Heck, I could write a better book than *that*." What usually happens next is that he proceeds to demonstrate that he can't write a better book than that.

From time to time someone—a student, a colleague, a publisher's representative—said to me, "You know, you really ought to write a philosophy text." I told him what I just told you in the last paragraph.

For ten years I resisted the temptation. So why this book now? It's very simple, really. I finally have something to say.

Like most practicing philosophers, I learned my philosophical techniques the way that those quaint villagers learned their native folk dances, by joining in and stumbling about until I got the hang of it. For ten years I've been inviting my beginning students to join the dance. "You want to know what philosophy is about?" I'd say. "Fine. Stumble along with me. After a while you'll get the hang of it." Frankly, it usually didn't work out very well. And finally it occurred to me that perhaps those students could use a little help.

So I didn't write another philosophy text. I wrote a book of elementary dancing lessons. It's intended to be used in conjunction with original philosophical works. Like all dancing lessons, it works best when accompanied by music.

One thing one typically does in a preface is to string out some acknowledgments. Well, I really don't have any, except, of course, to acknowledge in a general way all those excellent dancers whose movements I've tried from time to time to imitate. But what does Kant, say, need with an acknowledgment from me? I guess I could acknowledge the two thousand or so beginning students I've taught during the past ten years—for being so very puzzled at my dances—but their names escape me. Oh yes, I finished up this book during the first part of a year's leave financed by a John Simon Guggenheim Memorial Fellowship. I would have finished it anyway, but that sure made it a lot easier. Thank you, John Simon Guggenheim Memorial Foundation.

Writing a book of this sort is rather an extraordinary experience. I spent a lot of time fighting off the paralysis induced by real-time methodological self-consciousness. (You know what happens if you start thinking about *exactly* what your feet are doing in the middle of a dance.) Having come through it, I find that I now tend to confront my own creative work simultaneously as author and critic, as participant and witness. As you might guess, that doesn't make it any easier—but I'm beginning to suspect that it makes it better. So I am mildly heartened. Any book that helps *somebody* can't be all bad. Maybe it will even help somebody else.

I hope so. Rather a lot of help is needed, I fear. Nowadays, my beginning students come in clusters of about 150, and most of them seem to be concerned with getting past their humanities requirement without accumulating any grades which would jeopardize their chance at medical school (or something like that). I don't think that's entirely their fault. They're embedded in structures which don't allow them many alternatives. William Arrowsmith put it rather nicely:

> At present the universities are as uncongenial to teaching as the Mojave Desert to a clutch of Druid priests. If you want to restore a Druid priesthood, you cannot do it by offering prizes for Druid-of-the-year. If you want Druids, you must grow forests. There is no other way of setting about it.

Well, I can't grow forests. But I can write a little book of elementary dancing lessons—and maybe that counts as planting a seedling. I hope so. In any case, here it is. As usual, I typed it myself. Make of it what you will.

JAY F. ROSENBERG

Chapel Hill, N.C.
November 1976

PREFACE TO
THE SECOND EDITION

The Practice of Philosophy, it appears, has enjoyed a modest amount of success during the past five years—enough success, I gather, that the intrepid knight Profit Margins has gradually found himself beset and endangered by the ravening, bestial, and all-consuming Used Book Market. Thus it came to pass that the wise publisher, Sir Prentice of Hall, returned to the Wizard of Words and requested a boon. "How about a Second Edition?" was the way he put it, I believe. And so I decided to look into the matter.

As I said five years ago, sometimes a teacher orders a text for some class and afterwards says to himself, "Heck, I could write a better book than *that.*" What I guess I overlooked was the fact that sometimes the book in question is one which the teacher *did* write.

Upon interviewing students and colleagues about the text, what I actually discovered was that, while my little book of elementary dancing lessons was holding up *pretty* well, there were still a few steps that were giving the students a good bit of trouble. In other words, something more than *mere* economics spoke in favor of attempting a second edition. So I wrote one. The principal difference between this edition and its predecessor is that this one is *longer.*

In the first edition, for example, I briefly sketched the standard method of demonstrating invalidity by modeling—supplying an argument of the *same form* with true premisses and a false conclusion. That's nice, my students said, but how do we get hold of an argument's *form* in order to assure ourselves that our model has the *same* form? That, of course, is a *very* good question— so good, in fact, that I don't know of anyone who has an answer to it. So I did the usual next-best thing: I added a "sampler" of *common* forms, both valid and invalid. That now constitutes the bulk of the current Chapter 2.

Again, in the first edition I sketched out a dialectical process of meeting arguments by arguments, stressing the requirement that (as I there phrased it) "criticism must engage the argument"—the point being that mere disagreement with a *conclusion* offers no advance on resolving a philosophical dispute. Quite right, my colleagues said, except that our students often can't *distinguish* disagreeing with a conclusion from critically engaging an argument. Could you perhaps *show* them the difference? Well, perhaps I could. In any case, I decided to try. The current Chapter 4—a dialectical case study of the "Ship of Theseus" puzzle—represents my best shot at it.

Finally, as I continued to teach masses of introductory students, I found myself repeatedly talking about topics which, as I slowly realized, I *ought* to have mentioned in the text, but alas *hadn't:* meaning and definition, the use of analogies in philosophical thinking and writing, and the role of thought-experiments in dealing with claims of necessity and possibility. A new edition is a dandy opportunity to correct such oversights, and so I have. That's the current Chapter 7.

About the only thing that has been cut is my tortuous extended discussion of "infinite regress." The consensus that it bred more confusion than clarity was practically universal.

During the last few years, I've received some gratifying letters about *The Practice of Philosophy*—and surprisingly, not just from students of philosophy. The book, it appears, has not just helped *somebody* (namely, me); it's even helped somebody *else*. For the author of a textbook, that's terrific news. Five years ago, I planted a seedling. It seems to have survived. I guess this second edition can count as a *sapling*—and that's progress of a sort. Who knows? There may be a forest in there yet!

JAY F. ROSENBERG

Chapel Hill, N.C.
March 1982

PROSPECT

This handbook has two purposes. The more practical purpose, but in my view the less important, is to provide beginning students of philosophy with some useful guidelines for approaching what most probably will strike them as a thoroughly bizarre enterprise. To the typical beginner, philosophical practices often appear to be arbitrary, pointless, and trivial, and yet, at the same time surprisingly difficult and unspeakably frustrating. The more important, but less practical, purpose of the handbook is to try to explain why this happens, what it is about philosophy which produces these appearances.

Philosophy is different, in fact, from almost all other academic subjects now populating our universities. How it is different, and why, is the other half of what I hope to convey. Being different, a course of studies in philosophy makes different demands on students from those imposed by other academic studies. What those demands are, and how to begin to meet them (a sort of helpful how-to-do-it hints kit), was the first half. There is a third thing which I would like to be able to convey, but I do not think that I can. It is the genuine sense of liberation and joy which can be attained through the practice of philosophy. That, however, I suppose, is something which each of us must find or fail to find for himself. The most I can realistically hope for is that whatever I do succeed in communicating makes it easier to discover.

A few cautionary notes are probably in order. First, this handbook is largely concerned with technique. Consequently, sad to say, it is likely to be rather dry. It bears about the same relation to original, visionary philosophical writing that a carpentry shop manual bears to a finely crafted Chippendale chair. A moment ago I spoke of a sense of liberation and joy. But it isn't reading this sort of handbook that produces it, of course, any more than reading carpentry manuals makes beautiful chairs. What does the trick—if you're lucky—is mastering the techniques and putting them into action. And not only isn't that easy, but you're likely to make quite a few mistakes along the way, too. Chippendale's *first* chair was probably a wobbly disaster.

A second sad consequence of the focus on technique is that one rather quickly reaches the limits of what's teachable. The hard truth of the matter is that there just isn't any technique for creation or discovery. You can teach someone how to look, but not how to see; how to search, but not how to find. The topics of this handbook are the things that might be teachable—organization and exegesis, exposition and argument—techniques for processing conceptual raw materials. The raw materials of critical or constructive insight themselves, however, will have to come from somewhere outside all this technique. Critical acumen and creative originality can't be taught. At best, they can be nourished, enhanced, and matured. And for that, just two things have been found to help: familiarity with the lay of the land and practice, practice, practice. Both take time and discipline. To gain familiarity, there is no substitute for extensive reading; to gain practice, no substitute for extensive writing. This handbook does not provide the reading. It is intended, rather, to supplement such materials. In the Appendix, however, you will find some puzzles and passages intended to supply or suggest topics suitable for beginning philosophical writing.

A rather different sort of cautionary note concerns the *style of* philosophy shaping this handbook. At present, there are two main philosophical styles at large in the Western world, falling roughly on opposite sides of the English Channel. The Anglo-American style is often characterized as "analytic" or "linguistic"; the Continental style as "existentialist" or "phenomenological." (These are loose and untidy groupings, of course. Philosophers of both styles can be found everywhere, and the styles themselves intermingle and shade off into large gray areas not usefully branded with any single label.) This handbook is centered firmly in the analytic style of philosophizing. The sorts of issues, problems, and questions it regards as appropriate to raise and the sorts of answers it advocates and illustrates are conditioned by and reflect this underlying stylistic bias. There's nothing wrong with this—indeed, some stylistic decision or other is unavoidable—but, especially in an introductory work, it bears mentioning that there are perfectly respectable alternatives.

The choice of a philosophical style is only one of the individual commitments shaping this handbook. Every book has an author. In consequence, no matter how austere the subject matter or how dry and sterilized the academic prose, every book is conditioned by some individual's idiosyncrasies, prejudices, presuppositions, and ideological biases—if in no other way, then at least by what its author chooses to include and to omit. This book is no exception. It didn't write itself; *I* wrote it. Like most authors, I am a typically complex person with certain beliefs, desires, competences, ideals, preferences, goals, intentions, and values. Some of these commitments control what goes on in the handbook. Of course they do. I think that the ones which do are shared, useful, and rationally defensible. (That they *should* be, of course, is one of those values I was just talking about.) If this were, say, a mathematics text, it might not be necessary to mention that fact. It would go without saying. In philosophy, it is worth saying. What I want to turn to next is some of the reasons why this is so.

THE CHARACTER
OF PHILOSOPHY

What is philosophy anyway? Well, it's something that people do. It's a practice. More specifically, philosophy as a practice is an activity of reason. By itself, however, this says very little, for what characteristically human practice is not an activity of reason? Literature and history and science—all of these are surely activities of reason, but philosophy is neither literature nor history nor science, although it may be literary, historical, or (in an extended sense) even scientific. Practicing philosophers often present their thoughts in written form, but their business is not creative literary expression. They often discuss the views of their historical predecessors in their historical settings, but their business is not the scholarly sorting through of historical materials. And they often advance explanations and theories, but their theorizing is not, as is scientists', grounded in and in the same way accountable to controlled observation and experiment. What, then, *is* the business of philosophers?

At one time or another, almost everyone has experienced a certain impulse. Typically it comes as a feeling, a wonderment or an unsettling. And often it resolves itself into a vague but suggestive question: Do space and time go on forever? What if there isn't any God? What if there is? Am I genuinely free? Is anything ever really right or wrong? Are there any absolute truths? Is there really such a thing as good art? And, of course: What is the meaning of life? This impulse is precisely an impulse to philosophical activity. It is the wonder in which, as Aristotle said, philosophy begins.

Few people go beyond this point, however. The reason, quite simply, is that they don't know *how* to go beyond it. How does one think about such things? *Can* one think about such things? The mind boggles. One's thinking flounders, stumbles in tight circles, grows cramped and knotted. Eventually the moment passes, or is made to pass. Somehow the question is dismissed. It is postponed or rejected or repressed. And yet, a feeling may very well remain—the frustrating feeling that these are surely *important* questions, questions with important answers. If only one knew how to find them.

A practicing philosopher is, among other things, a person who tries to find them. It is part of the business of practicing philosophers to go beyond such feelings, to bring such questions within the scope of an activity of reason, to move them out of the heart and into the mind. It is part of a philosopher's job to make of such questions something that one *can* think about—and then to think about them. For this undertaking, philosophers must have both a general strategy—a method—and particular tactics—specific techniques for applying that method. And so they do. Philosophy, then, is an activity of reason with its own strategy and its own tactics, its own method and techniques. It is, in short, a discipline.

Philosophy as a discipline is perhaps thought of most fruitfully as being distinguished by its method rather than by a subject matter. It is at best exceedingly difficult, and at worst impossible, to give a useful compact statement of what philosophy is the study *of*. Indeed, one of the initially most striking features of philosophy is the multiplicity of diverse philosoph*ies* of various other disciplines—philosophy of science, philosophy of art, philosophy of religion, philosophy of mathematics, of history, of psychology, of law, of language, and so on through the whole catalog of human intellectual pursuits. Philosophy thus takes on the character of a sort of "second-order" discipline, one which has as its objects of study the "first-order" activities of the scientist, the artist, the theologian, the mathematician, the historian, the psychologist, the jurist, the linguist, and their many colleagues. If we insist on characterizing philosophy in terms of subject matter, then, the object of philosophical study in general might best be described as the rational, cognitive, or conceptual activities of persons. Seen in this light, philosophy as an activity is the application of reason to its own operations, the rational study of rational practices. Philosophy thus comes within the scope of its own field of activity, and, indeed, there exists the philosophy of philosophy (*meta*-philosophical inquiry) as well. "What is a proper philosophical question?" and "What is appropriate philosophical methodology?" are thus themselves leading examples of proper philosophical questions. And this is another reason why it is difficult or impossible to give a compact statement of the object of philosophical study. Any such statement, including the one I have just given, is itself the expression of a philosophical thesis, position, or view.[1]

The "second-order" character of philosophy can be highlighted by examining the kinds of questions which a practicing philosopher is inclined to ask. One helpful characterization of such questions divides them into two

---

[1] Charles J. Bontempo and S. Jack Odell, eds., *The Owl of Minerva* (New York: McGraw-Hill, 1975) is a fascinating collection of reflective essays by about fifteen contemporary philosophers on the topic, What is philosophy anyway?

groups—questions of meaning and questions of justification. Notably absent from this classification are questions of truth. Philosophers often find themselves confronted with a claim advanced by a practitioner of one of our "first-order" disciplines. A physicist might say, for example, that gases consist of molecules. An art critic might claim that Michelangelo's *David* is a more fully realized work than his *Pietà*. A theologian might state that God is merciful; a historian, that the underlying causes of World War II are primarily economic; a linguist, that the linguistic competences of humans cannot be explained without presupposing innate, genetically transmitted linguistic capacities; and so on. Now practicing philosophers will typically not be inclined to ask whether the claim confronting them is in fact true. If pressed, they are likely to decline to answer on the ground that they lack the special competences of the "first-order" practitioner necessary to assess the truth or falsehood of such claims. But they may well insist that there is some business which is their proper concern and which needs to be gotten out of the way first.

One species of question which philosophers in practice may pursue concerns the problems of understanding the claims advanced by "first-order" practitioners. What does it mean to say of one work of art that it is "more fully realized" than another? What are "underlying causes" anyway? Philosophers are constitutionally disinclined to take such "first-order" claims at face value. More typically, they will raise questions about what their face value *is*. That gases consist of molecules, for example, may look like a straightforward enough claim. But does a gas consist of molecules in the same way in which a ladder consists of rungs and sides? In the way in which a jigsaw puzzle consists of pieces? In the way in which a forest consists of trees? In the way in which a sentence consists of words? How can something visible—for example, a chair—consist entirely of things—for example, atoms—*none* of which are visible? Again, we know reasonably well what it is for, say, a judge or a parent to be merciful, but can a theologian who speaks of God as merciful possibly mean what we ordinarily mean? God's mercifulness, after all, is evidently supposed to be compatible with the existence of disease, drought, famine, war, earthquake, hurricane, and typhoon, and with all the diverse human sufferings which He apparently allows such calamities to visit on the innocent and the guilty alike. And that is hardly what we would ordinarily expect from a merciful being. Yet again, a philosopher may ask, do we have any intelligible notion of a "linguistic capacity" as something which can be genetically transmitted as eye color, for example, is genetically transmitted?

Second, a philosopher in practice may urge inquiry into the grounds—explicit or implicit—which "first-order" practitioners do or could offer in support of their claims. How can the gross observable behavior of substances, objects, and instruments in the laboratory legitimize physicists' claims about unobservable particles or forces? Can judgments of aesthetic worth be intersubjectively validated or are they necessarily nothing more than expressions of personal taste? Does the securing of theological claims require the existence of a special mode of religious experience, and can there be such a mode of experience?

Radical generalizations of such questions constitute what is most frequently thought of as the traditional province of philosophical inquiry. Thus philosophers will typically not ask after the grounds of this or that particular judgment of aesthetic worth, but rather whether judgments of aesthetic worth in general—or, even more broadly, whether any judgments of value (aesthetic or moral)—admit of objective justification. Nor are they inclined to take for granted the implied contrast between judgments of value and judgments of fact. Instead they will want to explore whether such a distinction can sensibly be drawn and, if so, in what it consists. Again, philosophers will inquire into the legitimacy of any inference from the observed to the unobserved, whether the unobserved be the forces and particles of the physicist, the private thoughts and desires of ordinary people, or tomorrow's sunrise yet to come. And, of course, the very distinction between what can and what cannot be observed will itself be up for investigation. And yet again, practicing philosophers will want to explore the limitations of perceptual experience generally, as a faculty yielding knowledge of a world independent of our experiencing it, not simply as one possible mode of justification for theological beliefs. Or, conversely, they may inquire whether theological claims can be validated at all, by experience or by reasoning. The practicing philosopher is thus a generalist par excellence. (My colleague W. D. Falk once said it this way: Ordinary people ask "What time is it?" but a philosopher asks "What is time?")

The activity of philosophy, then, whatever the details of its methodology—unlike the activities of "first-order" disciplines (or our daily business in the practical world, for that matter)—is carried on at one remove from the "first-order" facts. In consequence, it is a particularly rarefied and abstract practice. It is not an inquiry into facts in this sense at all but into the methods by which we search for such facts, the grounds or reasons on the basis of which we assert them, and the concepts we use in formulating them. Recognizing this allows us to account for much of what is peculiar and problematic about the practice of philosophy—the seeming elusiveness and arbitrariness of its methods, its often-lamented lack of a firm direction and of concrete results which can be looked upon as progress, and, more generally, the aura of unreality and detachment which non-professionals find so strikingly characteristic of the discipline. The roots of these appearances lie in the fact that philosophers are not in any straightforward way thinking about the world. What they are thinking about is *thinking about* the world. Such results as there are, then, do not take the form of new facts, but rather of a new clarity about what are and what aren't the old facts, and about their modes of legitimization.

Practicing philosophers are thus the very model of theoreticians and, since the objects of their theorizing are at one remove from the facts, the very opposite of practical folk. For the understanding at which a philosopher aims is not, as is a practical understanding, a condition of action. It is an understanding of the preconditions of those understandings which *can* shape our actions. Philosophical inquiry is not instrumental. It is not a tool. It aims at clarity, not as a means to facilitate action or to further independent life-goals, but simply for the sake of clarity. There is philosophical technique, but there is no philosophical technology. If the etymological characterization of the philosopher as a lover not of knowledge (*episteme*) but of wisdom (*sophia*) means anything at all, surely this is what it means.

A second traditional role of philosophy should be mentioned at this point. I have been speaking of philosophy as an activity which comes after the special sciences, which probes the foundations and superstructures of edifices already built. But it is no less correct to think of philosophy as something prior to science, as the mother of sciences. "Philosophy begins in wonder," Aristotle said, but this root wonder at the complex world in which people find themselves is the wellspring from which not only philosophy but all human inquiry flows. Speculation and theorizing about change and motion and the stuff of the world long preceded the organized experimental disciplines which we think of today as the physical sciences. Before there were physics and chemistry there was natural philosophy (by which name physical science still goes in England), and our sharp-edged disciplines grew from these philosophical origins as smoothly as the oak from the acorn. People theorized about justice long before any formal discipline of jurisprudence. People explored the possible forms of human society and its governance long before political science. Centuries of speculation about our human capacities to think and know and feel preceded the empirical study we now call psychology. And all of this theorizing, exploration, and speculation was and is fairly called by the name of philosophy. Newton and Einstein, Jefferson and Lenin, Freud and Skinner all dealt no less with puzzles properly thought of as philosophical than did Aristotle and Leibniz, Locke and Hegel, or Kant and Hume.

This historical role philosophy still preserves—at the cutting edge. Philosophy and the special sciences grade off into one another at the speculative margins. The theoretical physicist and the philosopher of physics, the political theorist and the political philosopher, the linguist and the philosopher of language, the theoretical psychologist and the philosopher of mind—all of these practitioners share their problems. Given my first description of philosophy, this should not be surprising. For it is precisely on the frontiers of any discipline that the characteristically philosophical concerns of sense (What does it mean?) and justification (How could we tell?) arise with special force and immediacy. The two roles of philosophy—as both the critical study of extant conceptual structures and the speculative source of new ones—thus complement rather than compete with one another, rounding out the picture of philosophy as our most general study of the nature and limits of human reason.

The history of philosophy—the great work of past philosophers—has a rather special role to play in this study. You will discover that a major part of the ongoing business of a practicing philosopher consists in the critical evaluation of positions and arguments advanced by other philosophers. This fact has led some to speak sarcastically of professional philosophical activity as being the curing of conceptual diseases which philosophers catch only from one another. But this too, it turns out, is nothing more than a reflection of the "second-order" character of philosophy which I have been stressing. Let me examine the grounds of this "professional inbreeding" in greater detail.

Two scientists may disagree at the level of their theorizing about the proper explanation of a body of observed phenomena, but they share the phenomena themselves as common ground. They may disagree about what a cluster of experimental results *shows,* but they typically do not disagree about what the experimental results *are.* Similarly, two historians may disagree about the interpretation to place upon a set of documents, but they share the documents themselves as common ground. They may disagree about what the documents *imply* (about why something happened), but they typically do not disagree about what the documents *say* (about what happened). And even two disputing theologians, at least those of the same religious persuasion, can find a common ground in their shared faith and, often, in their common commitment to particular sacred texts. So, in the "first-order" disciplines, when disagreement breaks out there is a built-in possibility of all parties to the dispute returning to an area of agreement and proceeding afresh from there.

But philosophers share neither phenomena nor experiments, neither documentary data nor faith. Philosophers operate, you will recall, at one remove from the "first-order" facts. What they do share, however, is a history, the common conceptual ancestry of the great philosophers of the past. Suppose, for example, that two philosophers disagree about the limits of perceptual knowledge, about what it is possible to learn about the world through perception. Now it is evident that they cannot return to a shared agreement about what is observationally known about the physical and psychological processes of perception. Their disagreement is precisely about what *can* be observationally known, not just about perception, but about anything at all. And although they may agree, for instance, about what practicing neurophysiologists say about human perceptual processes, such agreement constitutes no advance on the issue in dispute, for their philosophical disagreements infect both the sense of those neurophysiological claims (what to make of them) and their legitimacy. Where the disputing philosophers can find some common ground is in their shared conceptual heritage. For the great philosophers of the past—Plato, Aristotle, Aquinas, Descartes, Berkeley, Hume, Kant, and others—have all taken stands on the question of the limits of perceptual knowledge, and have offered arguments in support of their stands. The two disputing philosophers can thus find a locus for their disagreement in their differing attitudes toward one or some of these historical stances. And they can find the beginnings of a process which might resolve their disagreement in their diverse commentaries on and assessments of these views and the arguments mobilized in their support.

The history of philosophy thus plays a crucial methodological role in the practice of philosophy. It does not enter as an object of philosophical inquiry, but as the *medium* of that inquiry. It provides philosophers with a common expository idiom, a shared vocabulary of *concepts,* and a set of paradigms of philosophical reasoning, which can serve as shared starting points for contemporary reexplorations of central philosophical concerns. It is a rich stock of views and supporting considerations, to be sifted and resifted, assessed and reassessed, and—by the very best of practicing philosophers—occasionally added to.

The historical concern of practicing philosophers, then, will not end with an understanding of what their predecessors believed. It presses through to the crucial question of why they believed it. And the "why" at issue here is the "why" of argument, of reasons, not the "why" of, say, psychoanalysis or sociology. It is with the reasonings of their predecessors and not with their motivations that philosophers in practice concern themselves. Philosophical progress, at least in its critical dimension, is thus neither a matter of new facts and forecasts nor one of bread or bombs or bridges. It consists in such subtler business as refining a problem, attaining greater argumentative rigor, grasping connections, noting presuppositions, or seeing the point of a remark.

And just occasionally, if you're especially fortunate, these minute elements fall together momentarily and interlock into a larger visionary whole. And then you find the sense of liberation and joy of which I spoke.

2 THE FORM
OF AN ARGUMENT

About the methods of philosophical inquiry little consensus can be achieved. If, however, we attempt to separate issues of methodological substance from issues of philosophical style, there are a few points about the former on which general agreement might be reached. Probably the most fundamental of these is that philosophical views or positions require support by argument. By 'argument' I do not intend something essentially critical or contentious (although a philosopher can be as negative and quarrelsome as anybody else). In its broadest sense, argument is simply the giving of reasons for beliefs. If there is a fundamental ground rule of philosophical practice, it is that any view, however outrageous, may be introduced for discussion, provided only that its proponent endeavors adequately to support it by argument. So we need to have a look at arguments.

An argument may be thought of as a group or bunch or series of statements. In the cleanest sort of case, one of these statements will be tagged as the intended conclusion, expressing the target belief which requires support. Others will be marked as starting points or premises. The conclusion is what is argued *for;* the premises are what is argued *from.* The remaining statements will attempt to illuminate the connection between the premises and the conclusion, to establish that one who grants the truth of the premises is thereby committed to granting as well the truth of the conclusion (or ought consistently to be so committed). There is thus an implicit "iffy" claim that goes along with any argument: *If* one grants the truth of the premises, *then* one must (or should) grant the truth of the conclusion. An argument for which this "iffy" claim is itself true is called a *valid argument.* Validity is an "iffy" property of arguments. It is not, like truth and falsehood, a property of individual claims or statements. Nor, conversely, can an argument be true or false, although each of its premisses and its conclusion may be true or false.

Since the premisses, conclusion, and intervening steps of an argument are all statements, in the ordinary way of statements they may be appraised as true or false. If the argument is a valid one, then from true premisses it will arrive at a true conclusion. (That's what 'valid' *means.*) Suppose, now, that the conclusion reached in some argument is an undesirable one. You don't like it. You disagree. You believe that it's false or, worse, absurd. And so you would like to challenge it. How shall you proceed?

Well, it won't do simply to disagree, to claim—or even to point out—that the conclusion is false or absurd. Philosophical criticism may begin with such disagreement, but it can't end there. For philosophical criticism is *reasoned* disagreement, and there is an argument to be dealt with. Recall the fundamental ground rule: Every philosophical position must be supported by argument. It applies to your disagreement, too. In order to challenge a conclusion, then, it will be necessary to challenge the course of reasoning which supports it.

You may be firmly convinced that the argument isn't a good one. How could it be, if it leads to a false or absurd conclusion? But being convinced isn't enough. After all, the person who produced the argument in the first place is probably just as convinced that everything is quite in order. He may even grant that the conclusion *looks* false or paradoxical. "But," he is likely to go on, "the argument *commits* us to it." And if you continue to insist on the absurdity of the conclusion, the most he is now required to admit is that the argument commits us to an absurd conclusion. But it still commits us to it. In order to *escape* such commitment, however, the argument itself, and not just its conclusion, must be called to account. It's not enough to believe that something has gone wrong. You need to find it. In other words, you need to show *what* is wrong with the argument. For if there's nothing wrong with it—if you accept it—then you are committed to its conclusion, however false or absurd it may continue to seem. How, then, does one criticize an argument?

Well, what can go wrong with an argument? If the argument is a valid one, then from true premisses it will arrive at a true conclusion. If in your judgment it's arrived at a false conclusion, then one of two things must have happened: either it *didn't* begin with true premisses, or it *isn't* valid. This gives us two kinds of challenges to make. We can question the validity of the reasoning, or we can quarrel with one of the premisses. Let me take some time to look at each of these challenges in turn.

VALIDITY AND INVALIDITY: MODELING FORM

To challenge a premiss of an argument would be to challenge its content—the substantive theses from which it proceeds. In philosophy, this sort of challenge presents special problems, which I shall be talking about shortly. But an argument is more than a mere collection of statements. It is a collection of statements intended to stand in supporting relationships. Recall the "iffy" claim which goes with an argument: *"If* one grants the truth of the premises, *then* one must (or should) grant the truth of the conclusion." The conclusion is supposed to *follow from* the premises. And this, too, is open to question.

You may, in other words, dispute an argument's validity. You can challenge the argument's form. And you can do this even if you accept all the argument's premises. Whereas a criticism of content addresses one or some of the premises individually with the challenge "That isn't true," this criticism focuses on the *relation* between the conclusion and all the premises, and its challenge is "That doesn't follow."

The general theoretical study of validity and invalidity, of what follows from what, is called *logic*. Because of the centrality of argument to philosophical practice, logic is one of the philosopher's most important conceptual tools. As the result of the development of symbolic or mathematical logic in the twentieth century, logic has emerged as an independent professional specialty on the boundary between philosophy and mathematics. (And, as you might guess, there is now also something called "the philosophy of logic.")

Although much of philosophical argumentation is too elaborate to be reduced completely to mathematical forms, there is no denying that the feedback of symbolic logic into traditional philosophical concerns has produced considerable clarification, purging philosophical reasoning of many invalid arguments which had previously been hardy perennials. It has been particularly helpful in sorting out the valid and invalid inferences turning on the logical relationships of the quantifiers—'any', 'every', 'some', and 'none'—and the modalities—'necessary', 'possible', and 'impossible'. In consequence, students who plan to pursue the study of philosophy with some seriousness beyond the introductory level would be well advised to acquaint themselves with at least the basics of symbolic techniques. But since philosophers have worked with the concepts of validity and invalidity for hundreds of years in the absence of these mathematical tools, there is obviously a good deal that one can accomplish without engaging in such specialized studies. Let's next spend some time on these matters.

The critical fact about validity and invalidity is that they are essentially matters of the form of arguments, the pattern of relationships exhibited among various concepts. Thus, they are largely independent of the arguments' particular contents, the specific concepts entering into the patterned relationships. This is just what makes it possible to treat logical notions mathematically. It is really only another way of stressing the "iffy" character of validity: *If* the premises are true, then the conclusion must also be true. Surely, that is something we ought to be able to know about an argument without knowing *whether* the premises or conclusion are true. Facility with the logical assessment of arguments can be improved, then, by developing an acquaintance with and a sensitivity to recurrent patterns of reasoning. Even a short time spent in the study of philosophy will be sufficient to equip you with a fairly sizable stock of valid and invalid patterns on which to draw. But it would be useful if we had, in addition, a general approach to assessing the validity or invalidity of some, perhaps unfamiliar, pattern of reasoning in a philosophical argument—if not a conclusive mechanical testing technique, then at least a *modus operandi* which, properly pursued, might save us from an unwanted conclusion by successfully challenging the validity of the argument which seems to lead to it.

The characteristic of valid argument patterns which makes possible such a general approach is that they necessarily lead from truths to truths. This is just our "iffy" claim all over again: If the premises are true, then the conclusion must also be true. Conversely, if a pattern of argument *can* lead from truths to falsehoods, it follows that it cannot be a valid pattern. This observation gives us a handle on demonstrating invalidity. For we can show that an argument pattern is invalid if we can find another argument which has the *same* pattern but which proceeds from obviously acceptable premises to an obviously unacceptable conclusion—that is, to a conclusion which *all* of the participants to the original dispute would agree was false. This is the technique of *modeling*. You extract from the disputed argument the pattern of relationships underlying the passage from premises to conclusion, and you construct a second argument on that model which passes from indisputably true premises to an indisputably false conclusion. If you can do this, you have established that the premises and conclusion of an argument *can* stand in that pattern of relationships even though the premises are true and the conclusion false. It follows that the fact that the premises of the original argument are true and *do* stand in that pattern of relationships to the original conclusion does not, by itself, commit you to accept the truth of that conclusion.

An example should make things clearer. Here are two short passages from Descartes' first *Meditation:*

I. Everything which I have thus far accepted as entirely true and assured has been acquired from the senses or by means of the senses. But I have learned by experience that these senses sometimes mislead me, and it is prudent never to trust wholly those things which have once deceived us.
II. But perhaps God did not wish me to be deceived in that fashion, since he is said to be supremely good. But if it was repugnant to his goodness to have made me so that I was always mistaken, it would seem also to be inconsistent for him to permit me to be sometimes mistaken, and nevertheless I cannot doubt that he does permit it.[1]

We're not going to concern ourselves with the role of these passages in Descartes' larger project, or with the wide variety of philosophical queries which

---

[1] René Descartes, *Meditations on First Philosophy,* trans. Laurence J. Lafleur (Indianapolis and New York: Bobbs-Merrill, 1960), pp. 18, 20.

could be addressed to their sense or to their presuppositions. But each of these passages contains, or at least suggests, a little argument, and we are going to concern ourselves with these. In each passage, Descartes may be understood as proposing that something could always happen. In the first instance, he suggests that it could be the case that his senses always deceive him; in the second, that it could be the case that God always permits him to be mistaken. And in each instance, he gives a reason for supposing that this is so. In the first case, his reason is that his senses sometimes deceive him; in the second, that God sometimes permits him to be mistaken. So we may, without too much violence, extract two cleaned-up arguments from these passages, each argument having one premiss and a conclusion:

A1   My senses sometimes deceive me.

Therefore, it could be the case that my senses always deceive me.

A2   God sometimes permits me to be mistaken.

Therefore, it could be the case that God always permits me to be mistaken.

Once we have sorted out matters in this way, a little scrutiny suggests that we are dealing with two examples of a single pattern of reasoning. One way of representing the common form of these two arguments is to retain the shared features but replace the specific differences of content by "dummies," or placeholders. If we try that with A1 and A2, making a few grammatical adjustments, what we get is this:

A* X is sometimes F.

Therefore, it could be the case that X is always F.

If we replace the letter 'X' by 'my senses' and the letter 'F' by 'deceptive', we get argument *A1*. If we replace 'X' by 'God' and 'F' by 'willing for me to be mistaken', we get argument *A2*. We now have precisely the representation of the pattern of relationships between premiss and conclusion which we need in order to apply the technique of modeling.

What we need to do next is to produce yet another argument of the *same* form having an indisputably true premiss and an indisputably false conclusion. To put it differently, we need to find some other replacements for 'X' and 'F' in $A*$ such that the sentence we get by replacing them in the premiss is clearly true and the sentence we get by making the same replacements in the conclusion is clearly false. As it happens, this is an invalid form, and there are many possible pairs of expressions which we could make use of here. You may be able to think of some of your own, but here is one which occurred to me. Replace '*X*' by 'paintings' and '*F*' by 'forgeries'. What we get, then, is the following argument:

A3   Paintings are sometimes forgeries.

Therefore, it could be the case that paintings are always forgeries.

The premiss of *A3* is clearly, as a matter of fact, true. But the conclusion of *A3* is false. For a forged painting is a *copy* of some original painting, and it could not be the case that *all* paintings were copies. If all paintings were copies, no paintings would be originals, but if no paintings were originals, there would be nothing for the supposed copies to be copies *of*. So the argument *pattern A** is an invalid pattern and, in consequence, both of the original arguments, *A1* and *A2,* are invalid arguments.

It is important to appreciate exactly what we have shown here. In particular, we have not shown that the conclusions of *A1* and *A2* are false. Validity, recall, is an "iffy" property of arguments. So we haven't established that it couldn't always be the case that my senses are deceptive. And we haven't established that it couldn't always be the case that, despite his presumed perfect goodness, God permits me to be mistaken. To show either of those things would take yet another, still different, argument. What we *have* shown is that the fact that the senses are sometimes deceptive is not, by itself, a sufficient reason for believing that they could always be deceptive, and that the fact that God sometimes permits me to err is not, by itself, a sufficient reason for believing that he could always permit it. We have shown, in other words, that the conclusions of *A1* and *A2* do not *follow* from the premisses of those arguments, and that our accepting the premisses as true does not *commit* us to also accept the conclusions as true. We may accept the premisses and yet deny the conclusions without getting into any trouble. We have not determined whether Descartes' conclusions are right or wrong. What we have determined is that, right or wrong, he has not yet successfully proved his case. Consequently, even if we should grant his premisses, we remain free to reject his conclusions. (Descartes, of course, is not finished. He has lots of other arrows in his quiver. These were tiny excerpts.)

PRINCES AND FROGS: SOME CLASSICAL EXAMPLES

Skill in modeling argument forms is facilitated, of course, if you have some idea of what you are looking for, some idea, that is, of what the form of an argument *might* be. It would be ideal, then, if you could be supplied with a checklist, so to speak—a complete enumeration of all the *possible* forms of argument, one of which would perforce have to be the form of the argument which you were interested in evaluating. Unfortunately, that is just impossible. There are an indefinite number of forms of argument, some of them incredibly complex and convoluted, and there is no way to predict just what some philosopher will or will not come up with in an effort to establish his or her point.

What we *can* do, however, is to provide a sample of *some* useful and frequently-used patterns of reasoning—patterns which also often appear as *pieces* of those larger and more intricate arguments actually deployed by philosophers in defense of their claims. It will, in fact, be helpful to have some samples of both valid and *in*valid forms of argument—both princes and frogs, as it were—since, alas, philosophers are simply not infallible logicians, and so one does occasionally find a froggy invalid step in some philosopher's reasoning happily masquerading as a princely valid argument.

In deductive reasoning, what characteristically gets the job done (or fails to get it done!) are certain "little words" which signal logical relationships among the claims being made: 'if . . . then', 'not', 'either . . . or', 'both . . . and', 'all', 'every', 'some', 'none', and the like. We can typically discover our "logical skeleton" by looking for the patterns which such little words create, once we abstract from the specific *topics* being reasoned *about*. One way to organize an "argument sampler," then, is in terms of such little words, and that is the course which I will follow here. As my premises and conclusions I shall simply choose some dramatic "philosophical" claims. Since validity is an "iffy" property of arguments, it does not matter for what we are up to here whether those premises and conclusions are *actually* true or false, but you will surely have opinions about some of them. Perhaps you will even find yourself wondering how one might go about evaluating not just the *form* of an argument but its *content* as well—how, for example, one might usefully challenge the *truth* of some of these premises. That, I am pleased to be able to inform you, is precisely the topic of the *next* chapter.

1. IF . . . THEN

> IF abortion is murder, THEN abortion is morally wrong.
> Abortion *is* murder.
> _____
> So, abortion is morally wrong.

This princely valid argument form:

$$\begin{array}{c} \text{IF } p \text{ THEN } q \\ p \\ \hline \text{(Hence) } q \end{array}$$

is perhaps the simplest and most obvious pattern of correct reasoning. It goes by the classical Latin name *"modus ponens."* Its invalid froggy imposter is called "affirming the consequent":

$$\text{IF } p \text{ THEN } q$$
$$q$$
$$\text{(Hence) } p$$

For instance:

>IF the world was created by God, THEN it will exhibit order and lawfulness.
>
>The world *does* exhibit order and lawfulness.
>
>Therefore, the world was created by God.

We can show the invalidity of this second form of argument easily enough by the technique of modeling. Consider, for example, my dog Spot:

>IF Spot was a cat, THEN he'd have four legs and a tail.
>
>Spot *does* have four legs and a tail.
>
>It follows that Spot *is* a cat.

Both premisses of this little model argument are quite clearly true. Its conclusion, however, is equally clearly false. The argument, then, is invalid (since no valid argument could proceed from true premisses to a false conclusion), and its form—"affirming the consequent"—is indeed a genuine frog. (In the future, however, I shall mostly leave it to you to find your own models to demonstrate the frogginess of the invalid forms of argument I will be exhibiting.)

2. NOT with IF . . . THEN

When we introduce a 'not' into our 'if . . . then' reasonings, what we find is sort of a mirror image of the pure 'if . . . then' situation. Here, a princely argument looks like this:

>IF mental states are brain states, THEN they are located in space.
>
>But mental states are NOT located in space.
>
>Thus, mental states are NOT brain states.

In skeletal form:

$$\text{IF } p \text{ THEN } q$$
$$\text{NOT } q$$
$$\text{(Hence) NOT } p$$

In this case, the invalid froggy imposter is the form which mimics our princely *modus ponens* arguments.

> IF God were at all evil, THEN the world could be better than it is.
> But God is NOT at all evil.
> _____
> Therefore, the world could NOT be better than it is.

Or, in skeletal form:

> IF *p* THEN *q*
> NOT *p*
> _____
> (Hence) NOT *q*

Notice that it is important, when constructing skeletons for the purposes of modeling, that each occurrence of a word, group of words, or sentence be replaced by the *same* "dummy" letter every time it occurs—and, conversely, when you are actually presenting the model argument, that each "placeholder" in the skeleton be replaced by the *same* words or sentence every time that *it* occurs. Only in this way can you be sure that the model argument you end up with indeed has the same form as the argument you set out critically to evaluate.

3. BOTH . . . AND with NOT

The case of 'both . . . and' by itself, of course, is pretty straightforward. When 'and' is combined with 'not', however, we once again run the risk of confusing an invalid frog with a valid prince. The princely argument looks like this:

> Space canNOT be BOTH finite AND unbounded.
> Space *is* unbounded.
> _____
> So space is NOT finite.

(If you're curious, by the way, the first premiss of this argument is, in fact, false. I won't, however, say anything here about its *conclusion*.) When we skeletonize this valid argument, we get the form:

> NOT BOTH *p* AND *q*
> *p*
> _____
> (Hence) NOT *q*

Unfortunately, there is a frog in the vicinity.

> Mercy killing canNOT be BOTH morally obligatory AND
> morally wrong.
> It surely is NOT morally obligatory.
>
> So mercy killing must be morally wrong.

Here, our skeleton is:

> NOT BOTH p AND q
> NOT p
>
> (Hence) q

and while this may look deceptively like our valid prince, a little thought—
and a little modeling—should convince you that it is indeed a froggy imposter. (Consider, for example, that mercy killing might be *neither* morally
obligatory *nor* morally wrong. It might sometimes simply be *permitted,* for
instance, without ever being a moral obligation or duty.)

4. EITHER . . . OR with NOT

The case of 'or' is complicated by the fact that the word is used both
exclusively and *inclusively.* That is, sometimes 'A or B' has the force of
'either A or B but *not* both' (e.g., "I'll ask Abigail or Betty to the dance"),
while at other times it has the force of 'either A or B *or* both' (e.g., "Please
feel free to take seconds of avocado or beans"). Whether 'or' is used exclusively or inclusively, however, if we can rule out one of the alternatives, we
can validly infer that the remaining alternative does hold. In other words,
arguments of the form:

> EITHER p OR q
> NOT p
>
> (Hence) q

are always valid. As an example, we can take:

> Values are EITHER discoverable properties of things (like
> colors) OR they are conventional products of arbitrary
> human decisions.
> But values are obviously NOT discoverable properties of things.
>
> So values must be conventional products of arbitrary human
> decisions.

Notice that this argument proceeds from the *falsity* of one alternative to the
truth of the remaining alternative. We might also be tempted to suppose that

it is equally in order to argue from the *truth* of one alternative to the *falsity* of the remaining alternative. That is, we might be tempted to accept the form:

$$\text{EITHER } p \text{ OR } q$$
$$\underline{\hspace{3cm} p \hspace{1.5cm}}$$
$$\text{(Hence) NOT } q$$

and *sometimes* this will not get us into any trouble. In particular, we know we are safe when our two alternatives, *p* and *q*, are logically *guaranteed* to be mutually exclusive—when, for example, alternative *q* is simply the *negation* of alternative *p*—as in the argument:

> Judith's argument is EITHER valid OR invalid.
> As we have seen, her argument is valid.
> _____
> Hence, it is NOT invalid.

Nevertheless, we cannot accept this argument form as a true prince, for sometimes, alas, it can get us into trouble. Sometimes, that is, this form of argument *can* lead from true premisses to false conclusions. Indeed, it can do so whenever 'or' is being used in the *inclusive* way, as, for instance, in the argument:

> Our tests show that EITHER your generator OR your distributor is defective.
> Now your generator is defective.
> _____
> So your distributor is NOT defective.

Here, of course, it may well be the case that BOTH the generator AND the distributor are out of order. Only if we had an additional premiss (say, further tests) which excluded this third possibility would we be entitled to conclude that the defective generator was the *whole* of the problem. When 'or' might be being used in this inclusive way, in other words, what we need is not an argument of the form which we have been examining, but a more complicated argument—an argument of the form:

$$\text{EITHER } p \text{ OR } q$$
$$\text{NOT BOTH } p \text{ AND } q$$
$$\underline{\hspace{3cm} p \hspace{1.5cm}}$$
$$\text{(Hence) NOT } q$$

(And, if you are on your toes, you will notice that in *this* form of argument, the first ('either . . . or') premiss is simply superfluous!) What happens in any *interesting* 'either . . . or' argument, of course, is that we cannot tell just by looking whether the 'or' is correctly to be understood as inclusive or exclusive. Thus, for instance, in the argument:

> Sensations are EITHER mental OR physical.
> Sensations are mental.
> _____
> Therefore, sensations are NOT physical.

it is not clear that we can, without further argument, rule out the possibility that sensations are BOTH mental AND physical—and *since* we have not ruled out that possibility, the argument as it stands is invalid.

5. EVERY and SOME

'Every' and 'some' tend to be well behaved when they appear in premisses or conclusions by themselves. It is primarily when we combine them in a single claim about the relationships between two groups of items that we find an occasional frog peeking out at us from among the princes. This is easiest to illustrate with mathematical examples, so let us take our two groups of items to be the positive integers (1,2,3,4, . . .) and integers in general (including negative integers). Since -1 is smaller than every positive integer, the following princely argument is not only valid, but also sound—that is, it has a true premiss and a true conclusion as well:

> There is SOME integer which is smaller than EVERY positive integer.
> _____
> It follows that, for EVERY positive integer, there is SOME integer smaller than it.

Now it may look as if we were simply *repeating* ourselves in offering the conclusion of this argument—but therein lies the froggy peril. For consider the following argument:

> For EVERY integer, there is SOME positive integer larger than it.
> _____
> It follows that, there is SOME positive integer which is larger than EVERY integer.

Here, the conclusion does not "follow" at all! Rather, it contradicts something which we know independently to be true: that there is no *largest* integer (for we can always add 1 to any integer and produce a larger one). It is important, in short, to get our 'every' and our 'some' in such claims in the correct *order*. Whereas arguments of the form:

> There is SOME x which is R-related to EVERY y.
> _____
> (Hence) for EVERY y, there is SOME x which is R-related to it.

are valid, in other words, arguments of the form:

> For EVERY x, there is SOME y which is R-related to it.
> _____
> (Hence) There is SOME y which is R-related to EVERY x.

are *not*. Just remind yourself that

> For EVERY son, there is SOME woman who is his mother.

and remember that it is false that

> There is SOME woman who is the mother of EVERY son.

and you will never go astray!

THREE MORE USEFUL PATTERNS

As I have already remarked, the set of possible forms of argument is inexhaustible, and so a decision to break off a collection of examples at this or that point must, in the end, be a matter of judgment. We soon find ourselves wishing for some *general* tools for handling *all sorts* of arguments—and that, indeed, is precisely what is provided by the discipline of formal (mathematical or symbolic) logic. For me to undertake to present a mini-course in formal logic *here,* however, would unfortunately be an example of very poor judgment on my part. The topic is simply too complex to be usefully treated at such short length. Still, good judgment, I think, dictates that I not abandon the theme of argument forms without at least mentioning three more valid patterns of reasoning which are often especially useful—so useful, indeed, that they tend to show up very frequently whenever philosophers (and even nonphilosophers) set about to attempt to establish a conclusion.

The first of these patterns is characteristically found in "case studies"—arguments in which a complex situation is broken down into a series of alternative *possibilities.* If *each* alternative can then separately be shown to imply a certain result, then, although we may not be able to determine which of the various possibilities is *in fact* the case, we can nevertheless validly conclude that this result is itself true. When there are just two alternative possibilities, *p* and *q,* for example, the pattern looks like this:

EITHER p OR q
IF p THEN r
IF q THEN r

_____

(Hence) r

For example:

Human actions are EITHER causally determined OR mere random occurrences.
IF human actions are determined by external causes, THEN they do not arise from our exercise of free will.
But IF human actions are mere random events, THEN once again we cannot exercise free will.

_____

Therefore, there is no free will.

When the outcome of such reasoning is uncomfortable (as, perhaps, in the example), the argument is often termed a *dilemma*. The two alternative possibilities mentioned in the 'either . . . or' premiss are then called the *horns* of the dilemma. There are three things which you can do when someone threatens to "impale you upon the horns of a dilemma." You can challenge the *first* 'if . . . then' premiss—that is, you can grant the first alternative, but argue that the uncomfortable result does not arise from it. This is called "swallowing the first horn of the dilemma." Or you can similarly challenge the *second* 'if . . . then' premiss (swallow the second horn of the dilemma). Or you can challenge the 'either . . . or' premiss. That is, you can argue that the *enumerated* alternative possibilities are not *all* the possibilities, i.e., that something has been overlooked. And this is called "attempting to run *between* the horns of the dilemma."

The remaining two useful patterns of argument both establish their conclusions by reasoning from *hypotheses*. In these cases, one of the premisses is not *asserted* as something which the arguer is committed to believing to be true, but rather merely temporarily *supposed,* "for the sake of argument," to see what conclusions one could derive from it *if* it were true. As you might suspect, then, this is the pattern of reasoning characteristically employed when someone is interested in establishing a conclusion which is itself "iffy." In such a case, the argument skeleton looks something like this:

SUPPOSE p
·   )   intermediate steps
·   )   of an argument showing
·   )   that q would follow
·   )   from what we supposed
·   )

_____

q

(Hence) IF p THEN q

Here is an example:

> SUPPOSE that there exists some being (call him "Otto") who is omniscient.
>
> Now, it's either true that I will go swimming next Tuesday, or it's true that I will *not* go swimming next Tuesday.
>
> If it's true that I will go swimming next Tuesday, then (since an omniscient being knows all truths), Otto now *knows* that I will.
>
> And if it's true that I will *not* go swimming next Tuesday, then Otto now knows that I will *not*.
>
> So, in either case, Otto now knows what I will do next Tuesday.
>
> But the same conclusion can be reached about *any* of my future actions.
>
> So Otto now knows what all of my future actions will be.
>
> But then all of my future actions are already *determined*, and I am not genuinely free to *choose*, for example, whether or not to go swimming next Tuesday.
>
> ―――――――――
>
> Hence, IF there exists an omniscient being, THEN people do not have free will.

The second, even more common, application of such hypothetical reasoning is its use to show that a claim is *false*, by arguing that, if we supposed otherwise (that is, if we suppose that the claim is *true*), disastrous consequences would ensue. In this instance, of course, the "disastrous consequences" are only *logically* disastrous—that is, they consist in the derivation of some *absurdity*, either the derivation of a straightforward self-contradiction (often including the negation of the very claim we began by supposing) or, less dramatically, the derivation of some further claim which all parties to the discussion agree is simply obviously false. This form of argument, indeed, is traditionally called *"reductio ad absurdum"* ("reduction to an absurdity"). In skeletal form, such arguments look like this:

> **SUPPOSE** *p*
> -)   intermediate steps
> -)   showing that *x* would
> -)   follow from what we
> -)   supposed
> -)
> *x*   (an absurdity!)
>
> ―――――――――
> (Hence) NOT *p*

For our last example, let us travel to the island of knights and knaves, explored in charming detail, along with other strange territories, by Raymond Smullyan in his wonderful book *What Is the Name of This Book?—The Riddle of Dracula and Other Logical Puzzles* (Prentice-Hall, 1978). What you need to know about the inhabitants of this island is that knights *always* tell the truth, but knaves *always* lie. When you come across two natives, Ambrose and Boris, then, should Ambrose happen to remark "At least one of us is a knave," you could correctly reason:

> SUPPOSE that Ambrose is a knave.
> Then, since knaves always lie, what Ambrose said must be false.
> That is, it is false that at least one of them is a knave.
> But then both of them, including Ambrose, must be knights.
> That is, Ambrose must be both a knave and a knight. (An absurdity!)
> _____
> It follows that Ambrose is NOT a knave.

(And, parenthetically, you could go on to conclude that Boris *is* a knave, since Ambrose, whom you now know to be a knight, has truly said that at least one of them is a knave.)

Dilemma, argument from an hypothesis, and *reductio ad absurdum*—three useful patterns. But of course, as we have already several times remarked, there is more to any argument than its *form*. Every argument also has a *content*, a distinctive set of premises and presuppositions which are themselves being put forward by its author as *truths*. When an argument is formally impeccable but, for all that, still results in a conclusion which you judge to be false, then, it is necessary to come to terms with its content, to issue a challenge directly to one of those premises or presuppositions. How one goes about *doing* that is, as promised, the topic of our next chapter.

3 THE CONTENT OF AN ARGUMENT

CHALLENGING PREMISSES: BEYOND MERE DISAGREEMENT

The reasonably judicious and experienced philosopher, of course, will not often be found advancing straightforwardly invalid arguments. (Indeed, when a well-known philosopher did so a few years ago, it became a matter of some notoriety in the journals as his colleagues tried to figure out what the fellow could possibly have had in mind. "X's Logical Lapse," it was called.) Usually, the form of the argument, the pattern of reasoning, will itself be in order. If the argumentation leads to an unacceptable conclusion, then, it will be necessary to take on one or more of the premisses directly, to challenge the truth of the philosopher's starting points.

As with conclusions, however, mere disagreement is not enough. The mere denial of a premiss, like the mere denial of a conclusion, indicates no more than a difference of opinion. It is not enough to *say* that some premiss is false and should be abandoned. It is necessary to *show* that it is.

But philosophy, you will recall, is a "second-order" discipline. The practicing philosopher operates at one remove from the "first-order" facts. A philosopher typically lacks the first-order expertise needed to exhibit the falsehood of a premiss by direct recourse to data or experiments. What sort of challenge can be mounted against a premiss under these circumstances?

Well, what needs to be done is to provide the advocate of the premiss—the philosopher who offered the argument in the first place—with some *reason* for abandoning it. Here again, philosophical criticism is reasoned disagreement. But, given the "second-order" character of philosophy, how is one to accomplish that? There is one primary technique—and if you properly appreciate it, you are on the high road to grasping everything which is special about the practice of philosophy. The technique is to provide an *internal* criticism. You meet the philosopher, not in the archives or in the laboratory, but on his or her home court. You try to show that the premiss in question is one which the philosopher cannot *consistently* believe to be true. That is, you try to show that in the context of other accepted beliefs, the philosopher's acceptance of that premiss as true gets him or her into trouble. It commits the philosopher to something else—ideally, something explicitly denied, but in any case something which must be rejected. (Later, I shall look in detail at the various ways in which a philosopher can "get into trouble." For now, I shall simply illustrate one central case.)

The way you do this is by constructing an argument of your own— ideally, an argument whose premisses are a bunch of views, theses, claims, or positions all of which are accepted by the philosopher under examination (including, of course, the disputed premiss), but whose conclusion is some thesis which he or she clearly and explicitly rejects.

Let me go over this very slowly and carefully, for if you grasp it, you've overcome what is probably the major obstacle to understanding how philosophers operate. Suppose that philosopher 1 offers an argument which proceeds from some premisses—say, A,B,C—to a conclusion—T—and that philosopher 2 believes that the conclusion T is mistaken. So there is a dis- agreement. Philosopher 2 must now challenge the *argument* offered by phi- losopher 1. Otherwise there is *merely* a disagreement, but no evident possi- bility of progress. The argument, let us suppose, is formally in good order. So 2 focuses on one of 1's premisses, say A; she believes that A is false. Philosopher 1, since he takes A as a premiss, evidently believes it to be true. So the disagreement has spread; it has been transferred from T to A. But the object of the game is to get beyond *mere* disagreement. What 2 must do is to attempt to supply 1 with a reason for giving up A. So, in the most straightforward case, what she does is this: In addition to $A,B,C,$ and $T,$ there will be some other theses—say U,V,W—which 1 explicitly accepts, and still more—say X,Y,Z—which he explicitly rejects. Philosopher 2 attempts to select from the accepted theses some group which, together with A, imply one of the rejected theses, say X. In other words, she constructs an argument which proceeds from premisses $U,V, . . . A$ to the conclusion X. And if that argument is a good one, 1 is stuck. He must give up *something*. Philos- opher 2, of course, promptly suggests that A is what must go, thereby under- mining the support for T—which, you will recall, is where all this started.

But 1 has a variety of options. He may give up $A,$ but then proceed to offer *another* argument for T. Or he may let go of one of U,V,W. Or he can change his mind about $X,$ and make appropriate modifications in his other views. And there is still one more possibility—the one which is traditionally the most disheartening for a student to contemplate: 1 may criticize the argument offered by 2.

For, of course, things are never really as tidy as I've made them out to be. In the usual case, 2 won't be able to construct her rebuttal argument using *only* premises $U, V, \ldots A$, which 1 explicity accepts. Typically, 2 will need some auxiliary premises—say D, E, F—and 1 may take issue with one of these. Of course, to do that, 1 will need to construct yet another argument. And so it goes.

Several important points emerge from an examination of this pattern:

1. The initial disagreement between philosophers 1 and 2 is over the truth or falsehood of some, perhaps major, thesis T. But the requirement that criticism engage the arguments quickly causes T to drop out as a *visible* theme of the ongoing discussion. The actual battles will be fought at some remove— over, say, A and E.

2. Furthermore, as the discussion develops, it emerges that the actual clash operates not simply over the isolated thesis T but between two whole systematic structures of beliefs, in which T or its denial is embedded. For a dispute of this sort comes to an end only when one of the disputants cannot, by appropriate challenges and adjustments, get his or her *whole* position—acceptances and rejections—to hang together coherently.

3. But the most important observation is this: The discussion proceeds by meeting argument with argument. And from the very first step, what the challenge arguments are *about* is always some aspect of another argument.

Observation 1 accounts for the apparent *triviality* of some philosophical disputes. Beginning students in philosophy frequently complain that philosophers choose to focus on inconsequential puzzles rather than discussing important issues. Instead of facing the question "Is there an immortal soul?" they discuss "Can I consistently imagine myself witnessing my own funeral?" Instead of taking on "What are the limits of perceptual knowledge?" they ask "Can I tell whether I'm awake or dreaming?" Instead of debating "Are a person's acts free or determined?" philosophers consider "Does 'He could have done otherwise' imply 'He would have done otherwise if he had chosen'?" And so on. Frustrating as all this frequently is to the student, we can now see it as a consequence of the character of philosophical problems and philosophical method. For the big questions, the major theses, are sufficiently general and fundamental that they cannot fruitfully be engaged directly. Indeed, it is difficult to see what engaging them directly might consist in. Rather, they must be explored through their presuppositions and their consequences. A philosophical encounter, like a military campaign, is fought on many fronts simultaneously, and overall victory depends upon an extended series of tactical skirmishes and flanking maneuvers which inevitably and necessarily precede and lay the groundwork for any big push through the center. And not infrequently, when all these preparatory battles have been fought and won, the war is over. (Have another look at the quotation which is the motto of this book.)

Observation 2 accounts for the apparent *inconclusiveness* of philosophical disputes. Students of philosophy are frequently struck by the fact that philosophers argue endlessly. Nothing new ever seems to happen; there appears to be no progress. Instead, the classical positions of the major philosophers are continually being revived, refurbished, and refined. But, to the extent that this is true, it is not a shortcoming. It is not that contemporary philosophers are incapable of having new ideas. Rather, because the major stands on the large issues have generally already been mapped, the contemporary task often becomes one of attempting to work some of them into a coherent position. A contemporary contribution, then, often consists of the discovery of an unnoticed resource of a traditional position or of a way to meet some objection long thought to be decisive against some classical philosophical strategy. Of course, a dispute between two philosophers will always be conducted against the background of some shared beliefs and presuppositions, and there is usually a third party waiting in the wings, prepared with arguments to challenge them. The hard fact of the matter is that systematic philosophical views have a staggering scope, and the task of tying theses concerning knowledge, existence, truth, thought, language, action, and values together into a coherent conceptual package can hardly be overestimated. Quite often, the trick is not to give answers, but to ask the right questions in the first place.

Observation 3 accounts for the apparent *pointlessness* of philosophical disputes. Philosophers seem stubbornly to refuse to settle down and talk about the issues, to recognize, admit, and make use of the facts. They just keep talking about one another's arguments. From outside the profession, this looks like nothing so much as pointless domestic bickering. But you should now be in a position to appreciate that philosophical methodology demands this technique of confronting argument with argument precisely to avoid pointless bickering. The requirement that criticism engage the arguments is exactly a response to the need for a method which is, at least potentially, resolutive, which can press beyond mere disagreement and apply the leverage of reasoning in a way which affords the possibility of dislodging an entrenched philosophical thesis or view. The meeting of argument with argument is the essence of the matter. Unless criticism proceeded in this way, we would not yet have an activity of reason at all, but mere yeasaying and naysaying. And that would be pointless bickering with a vengeance.

THE JOYS AND PERILS OF DIALECTIC

The points I have most recently been making are sufficiently important to deserve a more extended discussion. We have seen that, even in the most straightforward sort of case where the acceptability of some claim is at issue, the methodology of philosophy already demands an elaborate sequential structure of competing arguments. The disagreement is transferred from conclusions to premises and from premises to presuppositions, ultimately pulling in whole complex families of beliefs and commitments. Much of what is initially disagreeable about the enterprise may become less so when seen in this light, the details of argument directed at seemingly inconsequential puzzles coming to be appreciated as tactical moments in a larger philosophical development. Ultimately, the challenge is not to this or that individual thesis but to the consistency and coherence of a whole family of beliefs in which the thesis is embedded.

It is not particular statements or theses, then, which are genuinely at issue in a philosophical dispute, but rather rich, more or less systematic *world views*. A philosophical encounter is like the collision of two icebergs. What lies beneath the surface is larger than, and gives shape and force to, what is visible above the waters. These philosophical world views have a special sort of comprehensiveness and elasticity. They shape our whole way of seeing the world. Opposition among them is *dialectical*.

Now the word 'dialectical' has had many uses in philosophy, from Plato to Marx. What I mean by it is not unrelated to these historical roots. A pair of world views stand in what I call dialectical opposition just in case they are incompatible but nevertheless are both tempting—there's an initial pull toward each of them; both pivotal—they serve as centers for ordering and regrouping families of beliefs; and both reformulatable—they are expressible by a variety of different specific claims or theses.

Consider, for example, what we might call the theistic and the nontheistic world views. Some people look at the world and see it as the perfect handiwork of a Divine creator, infused with a benevolent personal presence. Others greet this picture with incomprehension or hostility, seeing in the world only complex flows and interactions of mass and energy, the workings of blind and wholly impersonal forces. Perhaps most people have moments of both sorts from time to time, sometimes confronting the world as a deep mystery, with awe and reverence, and sometimes confronting it as a mere object, imperfectly understood, to be sure, but perfectly understandable and able some day to be grasped and mastered.

Both pulls are undeniably there. Both pictures have an undeniable attraction for us. But it is clear that, even with the most prodigious efforts at self-deception, one cannot retain both pictures indefinitely at the same time. They are ultimately incompatible with each other.

Now how is this incompatibility to be expressed? One traditional way, of course, is as a disagreement over the *statement* "God exists." One philosopher offers an argument for or against the statement; another replies with criticisms of that argument; the first responds to the criticism of the second with a critique of his own; still other voices enter the chorus; and so it goes. But to see this ongoing dialogue as a dispute concerning only the truth or falsehood of a single statement is to overlook the greater hidden mass of the icebergs.

For, in a sense, everything is touched by the issue. One of these disputants, for example, lives in a universe permeated with meaning. It, and we within it, have a purpose, exist for a reason. For the other, in contrast, if there are to be meanings and purposes at all, they will need to be human meanings and purposes, for we are here not by design but as the result of the random coming together of appropriate raw materials and the systematic evolutionary working out of this original fortuitous chance concurrence.

Again, one philosopher sees people as "a little lower than the angels"— as creatures who are imbued with souls and with a Divine spark of life, who are granted the freedom to choose between good and evil, in accordance with or in opposition to God's will. For the other, however, we are perhaps only "a little higher than the apes"—sophisticated deterministic organic data-processors which create whatever values there are in the process of our mutual interactions and our continuing adaptation to a universe of value-free, uncaring stuff. For one, our death is our transition to a higher life; for the other, it is only the ultimate malfunction.

Any of these differences, and many others, may emerge as a focal point from which the dialectical process of meeting argument with argument develops. People have souls—or they do not. There is life after death—or there is not. We have free will—or we are determined. There are ultimate values— or all values are conventional. Sensory perception is our only knowledge-yielding faculty—or mystical experience gives us access to a higher reality. Whatever the specific thesis, the ultimate aim of the enterprise remains the same—to assemble from pieces rooted in the preferred picture a consistent, coherent, articulate, and systematic whole which can withstand the test of critical challenge, to build a synthesis which hangs together under analysis.

From time to time, the center shifts. A thesis is reformulated. To the beginner this looks like yet another step in an endless and inconclusive process of regeneration of arguments. But, oddly enough, it is progress. With each such reformulation, more of what is at issue comes to light, more of the iceberg emerges from the water. Often the trick is to ask the right questions. Each shift of the center gives us more good questions to ask.

Even while the center remains fixed, from time to time the focus shifts. Argument turns to details and minutiae. Pointless hair-splitting, thinks the beginner. But this too is progress. For a complex and systematic philosophical world view does not simply fall to pieces. It has too much resilience for that. If inconsistency and incoherence are to be found at all, they will reveal themselves precisely in these fine points, in the inability of the whole to accommodate a telling criticism of some minute part.

That is how philosophical progress is made. And that is why it is so difficult to recognize. The dialectical process of philosophy proceeds by meeting argument with argument. Each criticism is a probe directed at a world view from within, a challenge to its *internal* coherence and consistency framed by one who stands himself outside it. And each response embodies

the mutual accommodation and adjustment of manifold beliefs, presuppositions, commitments, and convictions, an attempt to fine-tune the larger conceptual substructure which supports the visible thesis.

By now you may be despairing of ever entering into the practice of
philosophy in a significant way. How can one so much as begin a process of
argumentation which draws in these ways upon complicated systematic
philosophical world views? Well, it's time for a bit of good news. You have
at least the beginnings of such a complicated systematic philosophical world
view yourself. It is what you think of as "common sense."

Now a word of caution is immediately in order. Common sense includes, of course, a good bit of common nonsense as well, and one person's
common sense is frequently another's insanity. Nevertheless, there remains
considerable shared territory under the banner of common sense, and this in
particular is what I have in mind. Within this shared territory fall such
beliefs as these: that the world contains a variety of things—objects, plants,
animals, and people; that the things in the world have various properties—
shapes, sizes, and colors, for example—and exhibit various behaviors—some
grow and some move, for instance; that these things act on and interact with
one another; that we know about many of these things and about their interactions—we have met some, seen or heard or tasted them, and figured out
that there must be others which we haven't encountered; that we ourselves
think and speak and act in this world, and that our words and actions often
have consequences, some of which are desirable and some undesirable.

All of these beliefs, and many others, are what I think of as "common
sense." Common sense of this kind is everybody's starting place, and so it
will be yours. But the ground rules of the philosophical enterprise still obtain.
That a philosophical thesis runs counter to such common sense is just one of
those disagreements which serves as a beginning from which the dialectical
meeting of argument with argument must then proceed. Common sense is not
inviolate. It is not a final court of appeals. It is one philosophical standpoint
among the many that are possible. Indeed, *every one* of the "common-sense"
beliefs which I listed above has, in fact, been challenged—and for compelling
reasons—by some philosopher of the past.

And common sense has its liabilities. One typically does not have the
experience of putting its contents to the test of critical scrutiny. Since the
loose but interconnected set of concepts, beliefs, theories, and principles
which constitute common sense are shared working presumptions of our
everyday life, they are not, in the course of that everyday life, often challenged. Indeed, part of what students find so infuriating about philosophical
inquiry is just the philosopher's refusal to defer to and be content with common sense. It, too, must be put to the test of argument. Again, precisely
because it is not commonly put to that test, one typically does not know just
how to render fully articulate the structure of presuppositions and conceptual
interconnections implicit in it. Nor is one sure how much confidence to place
in its ultimate internal coherence.

But as a starting place, such common sense has its assets, too. For one thing, you're at home in it. You can usually recognize common sense when you hear it. For another, it has something very important going for it—it works. The conceptual scheme of common sense is generally a useful, practical framework for our everyday life and activities. And this surely creates at least the presumption that there is *something* right about it.

That common sense can and does function in this way as a more or less systematic stock of beliefs, theories, and principles which can be drawn on in critical or constructive argumentation captures what truth there is to the view that "everybody has a philosophy." But it does not follow from this that everybody is a philosopher. The decisive step toward that goal is made when one stops taking common sense for granted and puts it to the test. Recall Aristotle: "Philosophy begins in wonder." The great philosophers of the past represent, among other virtues, some of the most forceful, dramatic, and articulate challenges to our common-sense world view. And that is another reason why their arguments are still studied today and are likely to be studied for all of our tomorrows.

"THE SHIP
OF THESEUS"

A Case Study

So far our discussion of arguments and dialectic has proceeded at a pretty abstract and rarefied level. What we need to bring it a bit more down to earth is a good solid example of philosophical reasoning in action. So let us set ourselves a small puzzle:

> The ship of the ancient Greek mariner Theseus—let us name it "T"—is composed of 1,000 old, but still perfectly seaworthy, planks. Nevertheless, Theseus brings T into port for a *complete* renovation. The shipwright who accepts the contract has two drydocks, A and B, and he puts Theseus' ship into one of them, drydock A. Being a clever fellow, however, he recognizes that he can make good use of T's still-seaworthy planks, and so he sets his men to work around the clock according to the following scheme:
>
> During the first hour, the crew removes one of T's old planks and replaces it with a new one. In addition, however, they carry the old plank over to drydock B and set it in position as if they were beginning to *build* a ship in that drydock. During the second hour, the crew repeats the same process—replacing a second old plank from the ship in drydock A with a new plank and carrying the old plank over to drydock B where it is suitably fastened to the previously relocated plank. During the third hour, they repeat the process again—and they continue in this fashion for a full thousand hours.
>
> At the end of 1,000 hours, then, the situation is this: There is a ship in drydock A—call it ship "X"—which consists of 1,000 new planks, and there is a ship in drydock B—call it ship "Y"—which consists of the 1,000 old planks from Theseus' ship T reassembled into *exactly* the same arrangement which they had when T was brought into drydock A. Our question is: Which ship, X or Y—if either—is *Theseus'* ship T?

It may help us to envision what is happening in this story if we take a few "snapshots" of the process at its various stages. Let us picture the situation in the shipyards at the beginning, hour 0, in the following way:

Ship T

```
   o  o
  ooooo
   o  o
 ooooooo
  ooooo
```
_____   _____
Dock A   Dock B

The "o"s represent *old* planks. We will use "+"s to stand for *new* planks. The situation at the end of the first hour, then, will look like this:

```
   o  o
  ooooo
   o  o
 ooooooo
 +oooo
```
_____   o
Dock A   _____
                         Dock B

Jumping ahead to about hour 500, what we find in the shipyards now looks something like this:

```
   +  o                      o
  +++oo                     ooo
   +  o                      o
 ++++ooo                    oooo
  ++ooo                      oo
```
_____   _____
Dock A   Dock B

Finally, at the end of the thousand hours, what we would see were we to enter the shipyards would be this:

Ship X   **Ship Y**

```
   +  +                      o  o
  +++++                     ooooo
   +  +                      o  o
 +++++++                    ooooooo
  +++++                      ooooo
```
_____   _____
Dock A   Dock B

OK. What we need to know is which ship, X or Y (if either), is *Theseus'* ship, T. One way to begin is by surveying the range of *possible* answers to the question and, perhaps, narrowing down the set of "live options" to a manageable few.

When students first start to think about this problem, what they usually discover is that they have one or another of various possible *opinions*. Some of you, for instance, may be of the opinion that it is Ship X which is Theseus' ship T; others, that it is Ship Y. As we shall see, there is something to be said for each of these answers. Some students, however, are sufficiently baffled by their first encounter with the problem that they find themselves drawn to views which are rather less plausible. Some of you, for example, may find the problem of choosing between X and Y so confusing that you are tempted to answer that *neither* X *nor* Y is Theseus' ship T. And some of you may even be desperate enough to suggest the "answer" that *both* X *and* Y are Theseus' ship T. Unfortunately, neither of these alternatives fares very well before the court of common sense.

Indeed, the second of these peculiar "answers" can be dismissed on purely logical grounds. X and Y are *two* ships; Theseus' ship, T, is only *one* ship—and it is simply impossible for one thing to be two things. Of course, two things may be "identical" in the way that "identical twins" are "identical"—that is, "exactly alike"—but our ships X and Y are not even identical in *that* way. X, after all, is composed entirely of new planks, and Y entirely of old ones. There is simply *no* sense to be made, then, of the proposal that X and Y are both "really" *one and the same* ship, namely Theseus' ship T.

The proposal that *neither* X *nor* Y is Theseus' ship T does not fare very much better. Here, to be sure, we are not confronting a logical absurdity. But if we decide to go this route, we do inherit a rather nasty new puzzle, namely: What happened to *Theseus'* ship? It seems to have simply disappeared. If neither X nor Y is Theseus' ship T, *what became of T?* There may, of course, be an ingeniously convoluted story that can be told here which would have the result that we were dealing with *three* ships, X and Y and T—one of which disappeared as the other two came into existence—but if we follow the counsel of starting from common sense, that sort of story should hardly hold much appeal for us.

The upshot, I think, is that we can narrow our set of "live options" down to just two: either Ship X is Theseus' ship T or Ship Y is. And each of these answers, it turns out, has considerable common sense plausibility.

Someone who favors the first answer, that Ship X is Theseus' ship T, for instance, might argue as follows:

> Look, Theseus' ship was brought in for a complete renovation and it *got* a complete renovation. It was parked in drydock A at the beginning of the procedure, and—although lots of things were *done to it* while it was there— it stayed there for the whole 1,000 hours. As it happened, there were *also* some other peculiar things going on in drydock *B* during those thousand hours, but that's simply irrelevant to *our* question. All we need to do is to keep track of *Theseus'* ship during those thousand hours—and that's easy. *Theseus'* ship was in drydock A the whole time, getting a complete renovation. So it's the ship in drydock A at the end of the procedure which is Theseus' ship, that is, Ship X is Theseus' ship T.

Someone who favors the second answer, that Ship Y is Theseus' ship T, however, might offer a rather different set of considerations:

You'd certainly agree, wouldn't you, that if the shipwright had simply *moved* Theseus' ship from drydock A to drydock B right at the beginning, and then proceeded to construct a ship *just like* Theseus' from new planks in drydock A, that Theseus' ship T would be the one in drydock B at the end of the thousand hours. Well, isn't that more or less what actually happened? Of course, the shipwright apparently wasn't clever enough to just move T all at once—but he did move it *piece by piece*. What the crews did, in fact, was to slowly *disassemble* Theseus' ship in drydock A and then, just as slowly, *reassemble* it in drydock B. The fact that they were simultaneously using the partially-disassembled ship in drydock A as a sort of "blueprint" for the construction of a *new* ship is simply irrelevant to *our* question. All we need to do is determine where Theseus' ship wound up at the *end* of the procedure. Well, there it is in drydock B. How it *got* there—whether it was moved all at once or piece by piece—doesn't matter. All that's important is that it did get there. So it's the ship in drydock B, Ship Y, which is Theseus' ship T.

Now there are several interesting things to observe about these two answers. The first thing is that *both* of them belong more or less to "common sense." That is both a strength and a weakness. It is a strength in that it renders both of these answers *plausible*. Neither answer, in other words, is "wild" or "counterintuitive" or "off the wall," and apparently neither answer requires us to swallow any peculiar "metaphysical" principles about identity of the sort that philosophers are frequently accused of advocating. It is a weakness, of course, in that it renders both of the answers *equally* plausible. While "common sense" may feel quite comfortable with *either* of these answers, in other words, it is likely to get a little nervous when it notices that it is no *more* comfortable with one of them than with the other. (This, by the way, is one good sign that you are dealing with a philosophical problem.) And so a second thing to notice is that these two answers bring us more or less to the *limits* of what "common sense" can do for us here. It will be necessary, in other words, to begin to do some detailed *philosophical* thinking— that is, to attempt to engage the *arguments*.

For the third thing we need to notice is that these two answers are no longer *mere* opinions. They have become *reasoned* opinions. That is, each party to our little disagreement has not only expressed his or her opinion of what the correct answer to the question *is,* but he or she has also offered some account of *why* we should accept the favored answer as the correct one. And that gives us something to *do* beyond simply taking sides in the disagreement: We can change the subject! That is, we can attempt to examine and evaluate the *reasons* which each disputant has offered in support of his or her favored answer to the question. And when we do this, it is important to realize, we will no longer be talking about which ship, X or Y, is Theseus' ship T. As we shall shortly see, we will be talking about something else. We will, in fact, be talking about certain "common sense" views or, perhaps better, "principles"—not about views as to which ship is T, but rather about "principles" which each of our disputants is more or less *taking for granted* in concluding that this or that ship is T. And so the next thing we need to ask is: What *are* our two disputants taking for granted? What bits of "common sense" is each person *using* that he or she has, however, neglected explicitly to *mention?* It is time, in short, to "tidy up" the two arguments which we have been offered—to identify their presuppositions, their premises, and their steps, and to set them out in an orderly fashion. Let's next see how we might go about it.

The argument in favor of Ship X, we recall, focused on the fact that there was *some ship or other* parked in drydock A during the whole 1,000 hours. Whenever we looked, in other words, we would have found *a* (whole) ship sitting there. At the beginning, of course, the ship parked in A is Theseus' ship T. Now the argument in favor of Ship X grants that lots of things were *done to* the ship in A during the ensuing thousand hours. But what it clearly takes for granted is that no one of the things which was done to that ship was sufficient to change its *identity!* In fact, we can now see that the argument in favor of Ship X rests on the repeated application of something like the following principle: Replacing one part of a complex object does not affect the identity of that object. It is this principle, repeatedly applied from hour to hour, that is, which underlies our arguer's conviction that Theseus' ship T *persists* in drydock A from hour to hour. Tidied up, then, the argument in favor of Ship X (let's call it Argument X) looks like this:

1. The ship in A at hour 0 is Theseus' ship T.
2. Replacing one plank of a 1,000-plank ship does not alter the identity of the ship.
3. The ship in A at hour 1 differs from the ship in A at hour 0 only by having one new plank in place of one old plank.
4. So, the ship in A at hour 1 is Theseus' ship T.
5. But the ship in A at hour 2 differs from the ship in A at hour 1 only by having one new plank in place of one old plank.
6. So (from 2 and 4), the ship in A at hour 2 is Theseus' ship T.
7. But we can repeat this argument for hour 3, hour 4, hour 5, and so on up to hour 1,000.
8. So, the ship in A at hour 1,000 is Theseus' ship T.
9. But Ship X is the ship in A at hour 1,000.
10. Hence, Ship X is Theseus' ship T.

The argument in favor of Ship Y, on the other hand, focuses upon the fact that every plank in drydock B at hour 1,000 started out at hour 0 in drydock A and, what is more, that the planks in B at hour 1,000 are fastened together in exactly the same arrangement which they had at hour 0 in drydock A, when they indisputably constituted Theseus' ship T. What this argument evidently takes for granted, then, is a principle which we might formulate as: A whole is *nothing but* the sum of its parts. The arguer's conviction that Ship Y is Theseus' ship T, in other words, evidently derives from the observations that every plank in Ship Y was in Ship T at hour 0 and that, at hour 1,000, whatever may have happened to them during the intervening hours, those planks are again fastened together exactly as they were at hour 0. Put in our tidied-up form, then, the argument (let us call it Argument Y) amounts to this:

1. A whole is nothing but the sum of its parts in a determinate arrangement.
2. The parts of Theseus' ship T are the 1,000 planks of which it is composed.
3. The parts of Ship Y are the 1,000 planks of which *it* is composed.
4. But every plank belonging to Ship Y is (identical to) a plank which is a part of Theseus' ship T.
5. What is more, the *arrangement* of the planks composing Ship Y is (plank-for-plank) identical to the arrangement of the planks composing Ship T.
6. Hence, by 1, it follows that Ship Y *is* Theseus' ship T.

Like our two informal arguments, each of our tidied-up arguments apparently does lead to its desired conclusion. But, unlike our two informal arguments, Arguments X and Y both make explicit certain principles concerning parts, wholes, and change which their defenders are evidently taking for granted, principles which evidently played a crucial, if tacit, role in the reasonings which led to their differing conclusions. The most important thing for us to recognize now is that, if our attempts to resolve the disagreement over which ship, X or Y, is Theseus' ship T are to have *any* hope of succeeding, it is absolutely necessary for us to stop talking about those two *ships* and start talking about these two *arguments*.

It will not do, in other words, for the advocate of Argument X (or Argument Y) simply to *reiterate* his or her argument for the favored conclusion, or even to produce *another* argument which leads to the same conclusion. Such procedures may increase the advocate's *confidence* in the conclusion which he or she favors, but they carry us no distance at all toward resolving the disagreement between our two advocates. Nor will it do for the advocate of Argument X (or Argument Y) simply to insist that there must be *something* wrong with the opponent's argument. Of course, anyone who is committed to believing the conclusion of one of these arguments is also committed to believing that the conclusion of the other argument is false— and, *a fortiori,* that there must be *something* wrong with that other argument, since a valid argument with true premises cannot lead to a false conclusion. But to say only that there must be *something* wrong with the other argument is still to remain at the level of *mere* disagreement.

The crucial point to recognize is that, by saying only this, you are not yet offering any *criticism* of the argument. You are only asserting your conviction that the argument in question *can* be criticized, that is, that the argument is criticiz*able*. And, of course, if you believe that the conclusion of some argument is false, you will also *believe* that the argument which leads to that false conclusion must itself be criticiz*able*. A wholly sound argument cannot possibly lead from its true premisses to a false conclusion.

Actually criticiz*ing* the argument, however, requires that you do more than insist that there must be *something* wrong with it. What you need to do in addition is to give a specific diagnosis of *what* is wrong with it. And this implies that you need to look *inside* the argument, not just at its conclusion. You need to be able to find some premiss or some step within the argument of which you can say: "Here! *Here* is where the argument goes wrong. *This* is the false premiss. (Or: *This* is the invalid step.)" And you need to be able to back up these claims with *new* arguments—arguments which are not about Ship X and Ship Y, but about the premiss or the step which you have identified as the trouble spot in your opponent's reasonings; arguments which are designed to show that this premiss *is* false or that this step *is* invalid. That is what is meant by "Criticism must engage the arguments"!

Well then, how might such authentic criticisms look in the case of the two arguments which we have before us? At first blush, Argument X looks as though it will be pretty hard to fault. Apparently the only new principle which Argument X makes explicit is the one formulated in line 2—that replacing one plank of a 1,000-plank ship does not alter the *identity* of that ship—and, on the face of it, this is a claim which seems difficult to challenge. If replacing one plank of a 1,000-plank ship *did* alter the identity of the ship, then we'd never be able to *repair* a ship by replacing some damaged plank with a new one. Instead of the ship we'd set out to repair, we'd wind up with a *different* ship—one for which, presumably, we'd need new registry papers, licenses, and certificates of seaworthiness, since it would no longer be the ship we started out with. If we deny the claim made in line 2, in other words, it appears that we will need to abandon the common-sense distinction between changing something *about* a ship (which continues to exist after the change) and creating a *new* ship—and this seems rather too drastic a price to pay.

But is there anything else about Argument X on which its opponent might critically fasten? Well, interestingly enough, there is. There is the procedure of *reiterating* the application of the principle in line 2, that is, the procedure mentioned in line 7 of applying this principle repeatedly, plank after plank. Someone who wished to criticize Argument X, in other words, might argue that, while applying such a principle *once* is a valid form of argument, applying it *repeatedly* is not. That can lead from true premisses to false conclusions. One way to show that such a form of argument is *invalid,* as we know, is to construct a *model,* that is, an argument of the same form, which *does* lead from true premisses to a false conclusion. With a little ingenuity, then, a critic of Argument X might well come up with something like this: Suppose that Homer is a bushy-headed man—having, say, 10,000 hairs—and that once each minute we pluck exactly one hair from Homer's head. Now consider the following argument:

1. At minute 0, Homer is a bushy-headed man, not a bald one.
2. Plucking one hair from the head of a bushy-headed man does not change him from being bushy-headed to being bald.
3. So, at the end of minute 1, Homer is still a bushy-headed man, not a bald one.
4. But all we do during the second minute is pluck one hair from Homer's head.
5. So, by 2 and 4, at the end of minute 2, Homer is still a bushy-headed man, not a bald one.
6. But we can repeat this argument for minute 3, minute 4, minute 5, and so on up to minute 10,000.
7. So, at the end of 10,000 minutes, Homer is still a bushy-headed man, and not a bald one.

Given our assumption that Homer begins with just 10,000 hairs on his head, however, the conclusion of *this* argument is patently false. For the purposes of constructing our model, we can, of course, *stipulate* that the premises concerning Homer are true. If we are also convinced, then, that the general principle formulated in line 2 is itself true—and it certainly looks OK—we can conclude that we have found what we were looking for: an argument which has the same form as Argument X and which begins from true premises, but which leads to a false conclusion. And (if we have, indeed, done everything correctly in constructing this argument *about* Argument X!) this, in turn, will allow us to say *what* is wrong with Argument X: It is invalid. That is, there is something wrong with its *form*.

And what about Argument Y? Well, here too, it turns out, there is also some room for critical engagement. The implicit principle newly articulated in Argument Y, we recall, is that "a whole is nothing but the sum of its parts in a determinate arrangement." Now a critic of this argument is again not likely to be interested in claiming that this commonsensical principle is itself false. But such a critic might very well insist that the principle, as stated, is *incomplete*. After all, she might go on, some of the parts of a complex thing might *change*. Indeed, many complex objects—automobiles, typewriters, and the like—have *replaceable* parts. This does not show that such a complex thing is somehow mysteriously something "more" than the sum of its parts—but what it does show is that we need to pin the general principle down to specific *times*. The principle *should* read, in other words: *"At any given time,* a whole is nothing but the sum of its parts *at that time* in a determinate arrangement."

But now, our critic can continue, we can see what is wrong with Argument Y. It has a false premiss. It is not, however, premiss 1 which is false. It is simply imprecisely stated. The difficulty lies in line 4! For it is simply not the case that every plank belonging to Ship Y is a plank which *is* a part of Theseus' ship T. What's true is that every plank belonging to Ship Y is a plank which *was* a part of Theseus' ship T.

Being a part of Theseus' ship, in other words, is not an intrinsic property of some plank, in the way in which its shape and size and weight are among its intrinsic properties, but simply an *episode* in the plank's career. A plank is a part of Theseus' ship only at certain *times*. In particular, once it is removed from the ship and replaced by another plank, it thereupon *ceases* to be a part of Theseus' ship. It is simply not true, then, that all the parts of Ship Y at hour 1,000 *are* parts of Ship T. Of course, they *were* parts of Ship T, but, in fact, at hour 1,000, *no* part of Ship Y *is* (then and there) a part of Ship T. So, even though Theseus' ship at hour 1,000 is nothing but the sum of its parts in a determinate arrangement, we cannot conclude that Ship Y is Theseus' ship, for all of the planks composing Ship Y at hour 1,000 are merely *former* parts of Ship T—and we have *no* principle which allows us to claim that a complex object is nothing but the sum of its *former* parts, however they might be arranged. Argument Y, our critic can conclude, may be valid, all right, but we are nevertheless not committed to accepting its conclusion. For there is still something wrong with it—and we can now say *what* is wrong with it: It has a false premiss. That is, there is something wrong with its *content*.

And so it goes, argument and counter-argument. We began with two informal arguments about ships. We now have two new arguments—about arguments! The original question is not yet settled, but notice how the focus has shifted. To maintain her original stand, the defender of Argument X must now find an error in the new argument of her critic—and this will require her to search for *disanalogies* between her principle regarding identity through change and its repeated application in Argument X and her critic's principle regarding bushy-headedness through change and its repeated application in his model argument. And, analogously, the defender of Argument Y will need to search for challenges to the temporal restrictions which his opponent suggests must be imposed upon the part-whole relationship.

In this way, beginning from a small puzzle about ships, we can be led to rethink the vast question of identity through change and, ultimately, to make articulate our concepts of alteration and persistence, and of part and whole. This is dialectic in action. And if it does have its perils, as is now evident, it also has its joys—not the least of which is that it can, in the end, lead beyond mere disagreement.

FIRST
INTERMISSION

It's now time to pause and take a deep breath.

What I have been doing in the preceding four chapters is sketching out one conception of the philosophical enterprise—its goals, its methods, and the manner in which it progresses. The picture which I have been drawing is of philosophy as a "second order" discipline, one aimed not at enriching our knowledge of the world in which we find ourselves, but at the critical examination of our reasoned engagement with that world, the rational survey of our rational practices in the sciences, the social sciences, the arts, the humanities, and, indeed, in everyday life as well. The goal of philosophy, on this picture, is essentially to achieve a synthetic and synoptic *overview* of our place in the world—a coherent and comprehensive understanding of our abilities and limitations as rational knowers of that world and rational agents within it.

As we have seen, however, philosophical inquiry *in detail* frequently fails to reveal such systematic and global aims. On the contrary, philosophical inquiry in detail often appears trivial, inconclusive, and pointless—a series of sterile and irrelevant logical quibbles. I have also argued, however, that these appearances are in reality *consequences* of the "second order" character of philosophical inquiry, and in particular of the *method* which a discipline of philosophy's unique nature inevitably demands.

That method is what I have described as "dialectic." Its tools are *arguments* and its essential procedure is the critical engagement *of* arguments *with* arguments. We have, indeed, spent a good bit of time describing these rational tools and their application. We have seen that a critical challenge may be addressed either to the form of a piece of reasoning or to its content, either to the question of validity or to the truth of the premisses. We have illustrated a variety of common argument forms, both valid and invalid, and sketched out a technique of modeling by which validity can be called into question. And we have described the process of *internal* criticism of premises demanded by the dialectical and systematic character of philosophical views, theses, or positions—a process which ultimately challenges the *coherence* of some whole interrelated *system* of beliefs in which any specific philosophical claim is necessarily and inevitably embedded.

Throughout this discussion, I have continually emphasized the requirement that philosophical criticism engage the arguments—that is, that it address not simply the problematic *conclusions* at which some philosopher arrives but rather the *inner workings* of the pieces of reasoning by means of which he or she arrives at those conclusions—for only such a method, I have argued, holds out even the hope of *resolving* a philosophical disagreement. Whether one's critical strategy be the internal criticism of premises or the technique of modeling, then, what is crucial is that a philosophical challenger is invariably called upon to *produce* an argument of his or her own—a process which we have, in fact, seen in action in our short study of the "Ship of Theseus" puzzle. One philosophical view, then, is inevitably challenged from the standpoint of *another*—and we have noted, finally, that the loose confederation of concepts, beliefs, theories, and principles which I called "common sense" itself implicitly constitutes such a systematic philosophical stance from which a student might begin—although, as with any such stance, "common sense," too, is open to exploration, articulation, and critical philosophical challenge.

These, then, are the aims, the methods, and some of the complexities of the practice of philosophy. Philosophy, it turns out, is not a mere random clash of personal opinions but a coherent intellectual *discipline* with its own unique goals, tools, and strategies. With a preliminary understanding of those goals, tools, and strategies now in hand, we can proceed to a consideration of the larger structures in which those goals are sought, those tools put to use, and those strategies pursued—a consideration of philosophical inquiry in the forms in which you will encounter it and in which you yourself will be asked to attempt it. We can now turn, in other words, to the topic which in many ways is the centerpiece and motivating idea of this book—the philosophical *essay*.

PHILOSOPHICAL ESSAYS
Critical Examination of a View

The primary medium for the working out of a philosophical dialectic is the philosophical essay. This is a distinctive form which ranges from brief discussion notes in professional journals to works of book length. As a student of philosophy, you will (or should) be called upon to try your hand at writing philosophical essays. In any case, you will surely be reading some, and so an extensive discussion of the form is appropriate.

A philosophical essay is neither a research paper, a scholarly collection and arrangement of diverse sources (although the standards and forms of scholarly documentation should, of course, be observed whenever relevant and necessary), nor a literary self-expression. It does not deal with feelings or impressions. It is not a report or a summary. Fundamentally, it is the *reasoned defense of a thesis*. There must be some point or points to be established in the essay, and considerations should be offered in support of them in such a way that the considerations can be seen to support them.

Since clarity and precision of statement, organization of ideas, and logical rigor and consistency in the treatment of those ideas are primary demands of philosophical thought, literacy and sound literary style are essential preconditions of successful philosophical writing (indeed, I might add, of *any* writing). At a minimum, a philosophical essay should be written in coherent and articulate prose which adheres to the accepted rules and conventions of English grammar and composition. Enthusiasm cannot substitute for intelligibility, nor can a superficial facility with technical vocabulary effectively substitute for a sound understanding of the ideas and principles which such vocabulary has evolved to express. You should particularly avoid ponderous "academic" forms. Philosophy has had a bad press in this regard. Notoriously, philosophy is thought of as a "deep" subject. Well, deep it may be, but it is the deep lucidity of a glacier-fed lake, and not the deep murkiness of a mist-laden swamp, which should be your model.

Philosophical essays come in a variety of species. Each has its own characteristic structure. Perhaps the most basic of these, mastery of which serves as a point of entry to all the others, is the critical examination of a view.

The critical examination of a view, of course, presupposes a view to be critically examined. That is, you are confronted at the beginning with something which *itself* has fundamentally the form of a philosophical essay—a piece of writing in which some claim or thesis is advanced and in which considerations are offered in favor of accepting or adopting the claim. Correspondingly, a critical examination of a view may be broadly divided into two parts: the exposition and the critique. Exposition consists in setting out for study and discussion the view, position, claim, or thesis in question together with the structure of argumentation offered in support of it. Critique is the assessment or evaluation of that view through an examination of the structure and content of the supporting reasoning.

Views are usually somebody's views. The expository task is thus primarily exegetical. The business of setting out a position together with its supporting argumentation will usually be a matter of reading, understanding, and lucidly reporting on the content of some philosophical work. This undertaking has its own strategies and hazards, some of which I will discuss later.

As I have repeatedly stressed, the most important fact about a philosophical critique is that it does not end with disagreement. That is where it begins. Philosophical criticism is *reasoned* disagreement. Since the view up for assessment will be supported by its own reasoned considerations, a negative philosophical evaluation of a thesis requires that the arguments supporting the position, and not merely the position itself, be critically engaged. It is, you will recall, never sufficient to point out that a philosophical conclusion looks, or even is, false or paradoxical. If you wish effectively to call the conclusion into question, what you need to establish are the inadequacies of the argumentation offered in support of it.

As we have seen, there are two directions which a critical thrust may take. You may address the form of the argument—its validity or invalidity—or you may address its content. I have already said most of what can usefully be said about the first type of criticism outside of a course in formal logic. The exposition of the argument to be criticized is clearly crucial to this mode of criticism. The argument must be set out fairly and accurately and in sufficient orderly detail to allow for the extraction of a "logical skeleton" which in fact represents the pattern of reasoning actually being employed. Nothing short of familiarity and practice, alas, suffices to indicate what the argument is likely to be and how much detail is needed to uncover its logical structure. Even if you've successfully accomplished this rather tough job, however, your ability to demonstrate its invalidity is still limited by your insight in recognizing it for what it is and by your creativity in coming up with an appropriate model to exhibit the combination of that pattern with indisputably true premises and an indisputably false conclusion. And, as I remarked earlier, both insight and creativity unfortunately fall outside the limits of what is teachable.

Usually, however, you will be dealing with patterns of reasoning which are formally correct. In that case, your critique will need to address the specific content of the argument. The way you do this, recall, is to construct an *internal* criticism. You attempt to establish that the various premises and presuppositions used in the argument cannot all consistently be held together. You try to show that anyone who accepts all of those premises and presuppositions at the same time—and in particular, then, the philosopher who offered the argument in the first place—gets into trouble.

What kind of trouble? I spoke of uncovering an inconsistency or an incoherence in some philosopher's position. It is now time to talk about this matter in more detail. What kinds of incoherence or inconsistency are there? And what do they look like when you uncover them?

In a sense, there is only one *basic* form of inconsistency or incoherence—a self-contradiction. In the most straightforward case, a person contradicts himself by saying two things which can't both be true at the same time. At one point in the discussion he says $X;$ at another he says not-X. In a somewhat less straightforward case, however, he might say both X and not-X at the same time. This sounds a bit mysterious, but, in fact, we've already seen an example of it. A person who claimed that all paintings were forgeries would be contradicting himself in this way, for he would be saying in effect both that some paintings are originals (for the forgeries to be copies of) and that no paintings are originals, both X and not-X.

Roughly, a claim is self-contradictory if it is false and if its falsehood can be determined using *only* facts about the meanings of the words used to express the claim.[1] "Some parents have no children," "Tom is taller than Sam, who is taller than Tom," "Mary owns a four-sided triangle," "John is his own father's uncle," and "I met a married bachelor yesterday" are examples of claims which are plausibly self-contradictory in this sense.

Of course, philosophers are rarely polite enough to provide you with even this straightforward a self-contradiction. More often, the inconsistency, if there is one, will be merely *implicit*. The philosopher won't *say* both X and not-X. Instead, he'll say $X,$ and also say a lot of other things—U,V,W,Y,Z—which, together, *imply* not-X. This is the typical case, in fact. It's the one which I outlined earlier when I introduced the notion of internal criticism.

---

[1] My occasional cautionary phrases, such as "in effect" and "roughly," mark the locus of a philosophical problem. Some philosophers have challenged the view that there *is* a well-defined group of self-contradictory claims. The issue is a complicated one, but the gist of it is that the notion of a self-contradiction rests on an incoherent and unacceptable picture of meaning. The question has grown into a full-fledged philosophical dialectic, ultimately encompassing views concerning not only meaning but also truth, reference, knowledge, necessity, linguistics, and natural science. If you're interested in pursuing this problem, a good place to begin is Jay F. Rosenberg and Charles Travis, eds., *Readings in the Philosophy of Language* (Englewood Cliffs, N.J.: Prentice-Hall, 1971). The heading to look under is "Analyticity." As befits an introductory text, I shall continue, apart from this note, to be casual and intuitive about the matter.

Your job as a critic, then, is to make the contradiction *explicit*. As we have seen, you do this by constructing an argument of your own, an argument whose premises are claims which the philosopher accepts—U,V,W,Y,Z—and whose conclusion is something which he must reject—not-X. A main part of your critical task, then, is to draw out and exhibit the implications of what is explicitly said in the work being criticized. And that is another reason why a fair and accurate exposition necessarily precedes an effective critique. You can't determine what a person's views imply until you've first gotten clear about what the views in fact are.

But we're still not finished exploring the variety of subtle ways in which a conceptual incoherence may manifest itself. So far I have been talking only about contradictions between what is said or implied and what is said. In a sophisticated piece of philosophical reasoning, however, the inconsistency, if there is one, may well not lie that close to the surface. What a philosopher says will very often contradict neither anything else he says nor even anything implied by the other things he says. Nevertheless, it may still contradict something to which he is *committed,* not by saying or implying it, but by taking it for granted or presupposing it.

Everyone, of course, takes many things for granted all the time, and practicing philosophers are no exception. Some of the things taken for granted are what we might call *implicit premisses,* claims which are thought of as being so obviously true that they are just never mentioned. They "go without saying." Uncovering such implicit premisses is often a tricky job, rather like diagnosing the motive behind some act, but once they've been brought out onto the table, they behave just like explicit premisses. You work out their implications in conjunction with those of the other things the philosopher says, and attempt to exhibit the incoherence, if there is one, in the form of an explicit self-contradiction.

But even beyond implicit premisses, which may or may not be lurking behind a particular argument, there are some other things which are necessarily presupposed or taken for granted in the course of *any* argument. These are what you might think of as the most general ground rules for all reasoning. I shall call them "canons of rational practice." Canons of rational practice are the fundamental constraints which must be adhered to if you're going to have any argument at all—good or bad, valid or invalid. A specifically philosophical sort of criticism—and one which proves especially puzzling to the beginner—is to attempt to convict a person who offers an argument of violating one of *these*. Someone who *has* violated one of the canons has produced something incoherent, all right, but in a special way. He hasn't exactly contradicted *himself*. Instead, he's contradicted the presumption that what he's offering is an argument suitable for establishing its conclusion—or any conclusion at all. He has, so to speak, opted out of the game. Examples of such violations are clearly needed, so let me now consider some of them in detail. I shall, in fact, supply five.

FIVE WAYS TO CRITICIZE A PHILOSOPHER

1. EQUIVOCATION

William James reported returning from a walk to find a group of friends debating about a squirrel clinging to the trunk of a tree. As someone walked around the tree, it seemed, the canny squirrel edged sideways around the trunk, always keeping it between himself and the moving person. James's friends were quite sure that the person went around the tree. What they couldn't seem to agree on was whether the person went around the squirrel. Here is how James dealt with the question:

> "Which party is right," I said, "depends on what you *practically mean* by 'going around' the squirrel. If you mean passing from the north of him to the east, then to the south, then to the west, and then to the north of him again, obviously the man does go around him, for he occupies these successive positions. But if on the contrary you mean being first in front of him, then on the right of him, then behind him, then on his left, and finally in front again, it is quite as obvious that the man fails to go round him, for by the compensating movements the squirrel makes, he keeps his belly turned towards the man all the time, and his back turned away. Make the distinction, and there is no occasion for any further dispute."[1]

The moral of this story is that whether a particular claim is true or false depends, among other things, on how the words used to frame it are to be interpreted. Often, as in this case, there are a variety of different *readings* of some key word or phrase, and the same sentence may say something true according to one reading and something false according to another.

[1] William James, *Essays in Pragmatism* (New York: Hafner, 1948), p. 141.

Now it frequently happens that such a word or phrase crops up several times in the course of an argument. It may occur in several premisses, and perhaps also in the conclusion. Whether the argument is a good one, of course, will then depend, among other things, on how you interpret that word or phrase. If you read it one way, the premisses may come out true; if you read it another way, they may come out false. The person offering the argument, to be sure, wants all the premisses to come out true. Sometimes, however, the only way to accomplish this is to read the key word or phrase one way in one premiss and a *different* way in another premiss. To do this is to violate one of what I'm calling the canons of rational practice. It is to *equivocate*. A word must mean the same thing every time it occurs in an argument. That's the ground rule at issue. To violate it is, in effect, to change the subject in midargument.

A transparent, simple-minded (and sexist) example of equivocation can be found in the following little argument:

(1)   Only men can speak rationally.
(2)   No woman is a man.
            _____
(3)   Therefore, no woman can speak rationally.

Formally, the argument seems impeccable. The problem must lie in the content. One of the premisses must be false. But which one? That depends on how you read them. The key term is 'men'. Premiss 1, we might argue, is true: Dogs, apes, goldfish, flatworms, carrots, and the like cannot speak at all, and although parrots do speak, they do not speak rationally but only echo a limited number of phrases which they've been taught. If we argue in this way, however, we're reading 'men' as 'human beings'—and according to that reading, premiss 2 is false. Alternatively, if we read 'men' as 'males' in order to make premiss 2 come out true, premiss 1 will be false. But there is no *single* reading for 'men' according to which premisses 1 and 2 *both* come out true at the same time.

What we have in equivocation is, in fact, a subtle interplay between form and content: The validity of the argument is *itself* incompatible with the simultaneous truth of its premisses. In a sense, we have a choice as to what's gone wrong. Suppose we want to regard the argument as formally valid. Well, we can. We can view it as having the following skeleton:

(1*)   Only A's are B.
(2*)   No C is an A.
            _____
(3*)   Therefore, no C is B.

The occurrence of the same letter 'A' in both 1* and 2* indicates that whatever replaces it is to be read in the same way for each of its occurrences. But if we do that, as we've just seen, one of the premisses will be false.

Conversely, we can choose to regard both premisses as true. That is, we can treat the argument as if it went:

(1′)   Only humans can speak rationally.
(2′)   No woman is a male.
_____
(3′)   Therefore, no woman can speak rationally.

In this case, however, the skeleton of the argument will be:

(1**)   Only A's are B.
(2**)   No C is a D.
_____
(3**)   Therefore, no C is a B.

And this is a patently invalid form. (Indeed, the argument from 1′ and 2′ to 3′ is just the model we need to exhibit its invalidity, isn't it?)

So what's wrong with the original argument? Is it invalid? Well, it is *if* we read both premisses as true. Is there a false premiss, then? Well, there is *if* we regard the argument as having a valid form. What's wrong with the argument is that its validity is itself incompatible with the simultaneous truth of its premisses—and that violates a canon of rational practice. There is an equivocation on the key term 'men'. That's what's wrong with the argument. And now it is time for a full-fledged philosophical example:[2]

(a)   A necessary truth is true.
(b)   Whatever is true is possibly true.
(c)   Whatever is possibly true could be false.
_____
(d)   Therefore, a necessary truth could be false.

But, of course, a necessary truth cannot possibly be false. Something seems to have gone wrong. But what?

Let's think about it. Formally, the argument seems to be in good shape. It looks valid. (This is no guarantee that it *is* valid, of course.) Perhaps one of the premisses is false. How about *a?* It looks okay. If some claim is *neces-sarily* true ("A triangle has three sides" or "$2 + 2 = 4$" might serve as examples), then it's surely true. What about *b?* Well, again, there doesn't seem to be any problem. If a claim actually *is* true, then it certainly *could be* true. It would be self-contradictory to say that the same claim both is true

_____

[2] Taken from Paul Weiss, "The Paradox of Necessary Truth," *Philosophical Studies,* 6, no. 2 (1955), pp. 31–2. By the way, why would anyone *offer* such an argument as this? Well, one motive might be to show that there's something wrong with the notions of necessity and possibility—that the notions *themselves* embody some conceptual incoherence. Weiss's own motives, which have something to do with "illegitimate abstraction," are fairly obscure.

and couldn't possibly be true, for if it weren't even possibly true, then it would *have* to be false. But no claim can be both true and false, so if it's actually true, it must be possibly true. How about *c,* then? Alas, it looks pretty good too. To say that a claim is possibly true is to say that it could be true, not that it is true. It could be true—but it could also be false. (Of course, it couldn't be both.) For example, consider this claim: The snow was heavy on Mount Kilamanjaro this year. The claim is possibly true. That is, it could be true—but it could also be false. Even supposing that it is true, it still could have been false. (If the winds had shifted suitably, it probably would have been false.) If it couldn't be false, it would *have to* be true—but it surely isn't *necessary* that Mount Kilamanjaro underwent a heavy snowfall this year. So *c* looks all right too. What, then, is wrong with the argument?

The best thing to do at this point is to abandon the argument for a minute and think instead about necessity and truth. Before we began puzzling ourselves about the premises of this argument, we could think of sorting all claims into four boxes. First, we could divide them into the true ones and the false ones. But each of those groups admitted of a subdivision. Among the true claims, we could distinguish those which were necessarily true (in other words, those that couldn't be false) from those which were true as a matter of fact (but which might have been false). Similarly, among the false claims, we could distinguish those which were necessarily false (self-contradictions) from those which were false as a matter of fact (but which might have been true). If we call the claims which are true or false as a matter of fact *contingent* claims, we would have the following four kinds of statements:

NT:
> Necessarily true (e.g., "A square has four sides.")

CT:
> Contingently true (e.g., "Some tables are made of metal.")

CF:
> Contingently false (e.g., "No one has ever been killed by an atomic explosion.")

NF:
> Necessarily false (e.g., "George's grandfather had no children.")

Now we can get back to the argument. The question we need to ask is this: Which of these groups contain claims that are *possibly true?* Once we've sorted things out this way, however, we may notice that there are a couple of different answers. It depends, one might say, on what we *mean* by "possibly true." If all we mean is "not necessarily false," then all of the first three groups—NT, CT, and CF—contain claims that are possibly true. But if, instead, we mean "contingently true," then only the group CT contains claims that are possibly true. In other words, there are two readings of the key phrase "possibly true" to be dealt with here. Well, which one does the author of the argument have in mind?

The answer, of course, is both. He equivocates between them. Premiss *b* comes out true only if we read "possibly true" in the first way—as "not necessarily false." But according to that reading, premiss *c* is false. "A triangle has three sides," for example, is possibly true according to that reading—that is, it's not necessarily false—but it *couldn't* be false. It's a necessary truth. On the other hand, premiss *c* will be true only if we read "possibly true" the second way—as "contingently true"—for whatever is contingently true could be false. But then premiss *b* will be false. "A triangle has three sides" is true, all right, but it's not contingently true, and hence not possibly true either, according to *this* reading. There is no single reading of "possibly true," however, according to which both premisses *b* and *c* come out true. And, thus, the argument sins against the canons of rational practice. Its validity is incompatible with the simultaneous truth of its premisses. Its author is guilty of equivocation. And that is one way to criticize a philosopher.

2. QUESTION BEGGING

"But that's what you're trying to *prove!* You can't just *assume* it!" is a lament one sometimes encounters in the casual coffee-shop disputations of daily life. At stake is another canon of rational practice. The root notion is easy enough to set out roughly, but more difficult to make precise. Briefly and crudely put, an argument begs the question if it uses its conclusion as a premiss.

What's wrong with such an argument? Well, according to our diagnostic scheme, if there is a fault, it ought to lie either in the form or in the content. Now it's obvious that no question-begging argument is going to be formally invalid. Since every statement follows from itself, any argument which uses a statement as a premiss (with or without purporting to use other premisses) and then derives that very statement as the conclusion must be valid. It is impossible for all the premisses to be true and the conclusion false for the simple reason that one of the premisses is the conclusion and no statement can be both true and false.

The problem, then, must lie with the content. However, the problem in this case is not our ordinary problem of content. Normally, we criticize the content of an argument on the grounds that one of the premisses is false. But can we do that here? The key premiss is clearly the one which is also the conclusion. The only way to challenge the argument is to question *it*. (Any other premisses are, as it were, idle. The conclusion follows validly from itself without any help.) Well, then, is that premiss false? Essentially, the answer is that we don't know. More precisely, since the premiss is identical with the conclusion, the question "Is the premiss false?" is the *same question* as the question "Is the conclusion false?"

At this point, it is crucial to remember that any philosophical argument occurs in a dialectical context. There are two parties to the debate. One is the critic, who disputes the conclusion at issue. He believes that it is false. The other is the arguer. She accepts the conclusion at issue, believing it to be true. So far, however, we have only a difference of opinion. The methodology of philosophy exists precisely to provide the possibility of resolving such a disagreement. It requires that the proponent of any thesis provide an argument for her view, that she produce considerations in support of it. And it requires that a critic who wishes to challenge the thesis address his challenge not to the view alone but directly to the argument, to the structure of reasoning which supposedly supports the view. A presupposition of the *method,* then, is that a challenge to the argument supporting a conclusion must be *different* from a challenge to its conclusion; a criticism of the argument supporting a conclusion must differ from a mere disagreement with the conclusion. What we need to do is to turn this observation on its head: It is a presupposition of the methodology of philosophy that something *qualifies as an argument* in support of a conclusion only if a challenge to what's supposed to do the supporting is different from a challenge to what's supposed to be supported.

Now we can say what's wrong with a question-begging argument. A philosopher who offers it violates a canon of rational practice: The philosopher contradicts a presupposition of the very method which he or she professes to employ. What is offered as an argument in support of the conclusion does not qualify as such an argument according to the methodological requirements of the philosophical discipline he or she is supposed to be practicing. It does not qualify as such an argument because, as we have seen, the only way to challenge the supposed argument is to question its key premiss—and that is exactly the same question as the one which challenges its conclusion. The philosopher who advances such an argument, then, opts out of the game.

Criticizing an argument as being question-begging is a difficult and subtle business, for a philosopher is rarely unsophisticated enough to take the intended conclusion as an explicit premiss. If the conclusion is used as a premiss at all, it is much more likely to be merely implicit in the argument. And as I have already noted, the unearthing of implicit premisses is a sensitive matter of conceptual archeology, one that requires the sort of insightful understanding of the forms of argument which comes only through extended practice and familiarity.

The issue of question begging is further complicated by the fact that there is a sense in which the conclusion of any good argument is "contained in" its premisses. It is "contained in" them precisely in that it is implied by them. If the premisses are true, then the conclusion must also be true. Thus, for valid arguments, *settling* the question of the truth of the premisses always counts as *settling* the question of the truth of the conclusion. One must take care not to confuse this coincidence of answers with the identity of questions which constitutes the fallacy of question begging.

Indeed, it is sometimes dialectically appropriate to take as a premiss some claim which is *logically equivalent* to the intended conclusion. Two statements are logically equivalent just in case they imply one another. For example, these statements are logically equivalent:

> Every four-legged animal has fur.
> No animal with four legs fails to have fur.

So are these:

> If we invite Jon, we've also got to invite Susan.
> We can't invite Jon unless we invite Susan too.

If either member of the pair is true, it follows that the other is true as well. In this sense, they "say the same thing."

It will be dialectically appropriate to take one of a pair of logically equivalent statements as a premiss and the other as a conclusion just in case the point of the argument is to *demonstrate* the supposed logical equivalence itself. Such an argument frequently occurs in the critical movement of the dialectic. A critic attempts to establish that some philosopher has indeed contradicted himself by trying to show that something the philosopher accepted is in fact equivalent to something he's denied. The critic takes one of the claims at issue as a premiss and attempts to exhibit a series of valid moves which transform it into the other claim. She intends the premiss and conclusion of her argument to "say the same thing" because her proposed *dialectical* conclusion is precisely that they *do* "say the same thing." Her derivation of the logically equivalent conclusion, then, is actually a stop along the way toward establishing her overall critical claim—that the premiss and conclusion of her first-level argument *are* logically equivalent. The conclusion which the original philosopher must challenge, then, is this second-level claim, the critic's dialectical conclusion. And a challenge to this conclusion is a challenge not to the premiss of the critic's first-level argument—indeed, the first philosopher has already accepted that premiss in his original argument—but to its form, to the validity of the moves which are supposed to exhibit the claimed equivalence. Despite appearances, then, the critic's argument in such a case is not question begging after all. (And appearances can be very deceptive here. Most philosophers aren't as explicit—or clear—about what they're up to dialectically as they perhaps ought to be.) This highlights, perhaps as well as anything can, the crucial importance of the *dialectical setting* of a philosophical argument. That is yet another reason why the history of philosophy is methodologically central to its practice. It exhibits philosophical theses in a variety of diverse dialectical environments. And as we have just seen, the same thesis—indeed, even the same argument—can be subject to quite different interpretations and assessments in different dialectical settings. (We'll have some more examples of this phenomenon in a short while.)

For the reasons which I've just been discussing, genuine examples of question-begging philosophical arguments are not very easy to come by. Perhaps we can find one such example, however, in some argumentation surrounding the classical problem of *induction*.

In one of its guises, the problem of induction concerns the grounds for forming reasonable expectations about the future. All of us have such expectations, in fact, and it seems that we form them by generalizing from our past experiences. The sun has risen regularly each day, the traditional example goes, and so, unless we have some quite special reason to think otherwise, it is reasonable to expect it to go on doing so. We expect water to stay liquid at temperatures above zero degrees centigrade, and trees to lose their leaves in the fall and to grow leaves of the same kind the next spring. We expect ourselves to wake up in the same bed in which we went to sleep the night before, and to be much the same as we were the night before—more rested, perhaps, but the same sex and size and age and weight and with the same skills and failings.

But why *should* you expect such things? Why should you be *surprised* if, like Gregor Samsa in Kafka's *Metamorphosis,* you awoke one morning to discover that you had become a giant cockroach? What makes that any less likely than waking up to discover yourself much the same as you were the preceding night?

These questions form the starting point for a full-fledged philosophical dialectic. The initial response to them is likely to be something like this: The fact is that people just *don't* go to bed as humans and wake up as cockroaches. If sometimes they did and sometimes they didn't, then I'd admit that when I went to bed at night I wouldn't know what to expect the next morning. But, in fact, I go to bed each night expecting to wake up much the same in the morning, and I *do* wake up much the same in the morning. It's *reasonable* to expect to do so, then, because that expectation invariably proves correct. And this is true in general. What shows our expectations about the future to be reasonable is the fact that they work. Our expectations are regularly confirmed by experience. What could be more reasonable than that?

Now a response such as that is open to the charge of question begging. Here, with a slightly different emphasis, is how Bertrand Russell puts this charge:

It has been argued that we have reason to know that the future will resemble the past, because what was the future has constantly become the past, so that we really have experience of the future, namely of times which were formerly future, which we may call past futures. But such an argument really begs the very question at issue. We have experience of past futures, but not of future futures, and the question is: Will future futures resemble past futures? This question is not to be answered by an argument which starts from past futures alone.[3]

In our initial response, the claim is that our expectations about the future are shown to be reasonable by the fact that they work. They are regularly confirmed by experience. But are they? Well, we might grant that they always *have been*. But will they continue to be? We *expect* them to be, of course, but that is an expectation about the future. The response simply assumes that it is a reasonable expectation. The issue in dispute, however, is whether *any* expectations about the future are reasonable. And so the response begs the question.

Instead of Russell's "past futures" and "future futures," we have here our past expectations and our future expectations. But the critical point is the same. The question is whether any of our expectations are reasonable. The response points out that any expectation which works is reasonable and that our past expectations have worked. Will our future expectations also work? We can't say for sure, of course, but the response takes it for granted that it is, in any case, reasonable to *expect* our future expectations to work. But that is supposing at least one expectation to be reasonable. An argument which uses that premiss to conclude that some expectations are reasonable uses its own conclusion as a premiss, and thus violates the canons of rational practice. Our responder is guilty of question begging. And that is a second way to criticize a philosopher.

3. INFINITE REGRESS

Beginning students in philosophy—and even some more advanced ones—are often rather intimidated by the word "infinite." They tend to think of Infinity as a *big thing*, big enough to deserve a capital letter—so big, in fact, that people can't quite wrap their minds around it. "The Infinite is beyond human comprehension" is how the story goes.

Well, the pleasant truth of the matter is that there isn't a *thing* called "Infinity" or "the Infinite." (Of course, some philosopher might introduce such a thing into his world view—and he would then owe us an account of what he was talking about. But that comes later.) The word which does the work is not the noun "infinity" or *"the* infinite," but rather the adjective "in-

[3] Bertrand Russell, *The Problems of Philosophy* (New York: Oxford University Press, 1959), pp. 64–5.

finite." Infinity is not a thing—but there are infinite things. This may still sound a bit intimidating, so let me remind you of one of them which is an old friend of yours.

The series of positive integers

$$1, \quad 2, \quad 3, \quad 4, \quad 5, \quad . \quad . \quad .$$

is a familiar example of an infinite sequence. In general, the things that are infinite are things like sequences, series, sets, classes, groups, and collections—things that are composed of a plurality of elements or members. Whether or not such a thing is infinite depends upon *how many* members it has. The series of positive integers has an infinite number of members.[4] Infinity, so to speak, is not a "super number" *in* the sequence. It's a number *of* the sequence, a commentary on how many members it contains.

The sequence of positive integers has no last (highest) member. As we progress along the sequence, we never reach an ending point—not because it is "too far away" but because there *isn't* any. Analogously, the sequence of negative integers has no first (lowest) member:

$$. \quad . \quad . \quad , \quad -5, \quad -4, \quad -3, \quad -2, \quad -1$$

As we *regress* (travel back) along the sequence, we never reach a beginning point—again, not because it is "too far away" but because there isn't any. Some infinite collections, of course, aren't ordered, as the integers are. But from such an unordered set or collection of elements there will always be an infinite number of ways to select elements one by one—e_1, e_2, e_3, . . .—and *put* them in a sequence which matches up with, for example, the integers:

$$1, \quad 2, \quad 3, \quad 4, \quad 5, \quad . \quad . \quad .$$

$$e_1, \quad e_2, \quad e_3, \quad e_4, \quad e_5, \quad . \quad . \quad .$$

What unifies these various examples of infinite things is the notion of a nonterminating process—a procedure for progressing or regressing along a sequence or for selecting elements from an unordered collection which does not come to an end. At each step there is a rule for taking the next step—but there is no rule for stopping. Nonterminating processes can crop up in diverse places. Perpetual check in chess is an example of such a process. (A special stopping rule had to be added to the rules of chess in order to guarantee that every game would necessarily come to an end sooner or later.)

---

[4] More precisely, it has a *denumerably* or *countably* infinite number of members. Not all infinite collections are the "same size," a puzzling claim that is explored and made precise in a branch of mathematics called "transfinite arithmetic."

An infinite regress of the sort that interests philosophers is a non-terminating *rational* process—a process of drawing conclusions, giving reasons, explaining, justifying, deriving, and so on. Now there is nothing wrong with nonterminating rational processes in general. Suppose, for example, that Tom is tall. It is perfectly possible to derive, step by step, an infinite number of (completely uninteresting) necessary consequences from this supposition. Let '(1)' abbreviate "Tom is tall." Then from (1), it follows that

(2)
    It is true that (1).

and

(3)
    It is true that (2).

and

(4)
    It is true that (3).

And so on without end (*ad infinitum* or "to infinity," as the Latin has it). All of these consequences are terribly dull, of course, but mere tediousness carries no philosophical weight, either for or against an argument.

In order for the discovery of a nonterminating rational process to have a critical bearing on a philosophical view or thesis, some additional conditions must obtain. To begin with, the process must be a *regress:* It must dictate that some further step must always be taken *before* any given step can be taken. Second, the proposed regress must be a genuine consequence of the philosophical view or thesis being criticized. Third, and even more important, there must be something *wrong* about this uncovered infinite process. Its existence must constitute an incoherence in the overall philosophical position from which it has been derived. Here's a comparatively simple example, drawn from philosophical reflection on moral agency.

A traditional and plausible view concerning moral responsibility is that a person can justifiably be held to account only for those actions which are in his or her control. If my behavior results from drugs or hypnosis, bodily manipulation by implanted electrodes or a team of hefty wrestlers, or a knee-jerk kind of reflex, neither praise nor blame attaches to it. Only what one does voluntarily, only one's voluntary acts are legitimately open for moral appraisal. And so the questions naturally arise: Which acts are *voluntary* acts? In what does the voluntariness of an act consist?

A classical answer to this question is that the voluntariness of an act consists in the act's having a special kind of *cause*. One is responsible only for what one does "of one's own free will." A voluntary act, then, is one caused by a volition or *act of will*. What excuses my behavior in the cases listed above is that what I do is not something I *will* to do. My behavior is not caused by an act of my will but by chemical reactions or electrical discharges or the hypnotist's commands. But I can be held morally account-able only for what I will to do, only for the behavior which does result from acts of my will. So, in such cases, I am off the hook.

Let us call this the Volitionist theory. The critical response to this theory begins by uncovering an infinite regress. Consider these acts of will themselves. Are they voluntary or involuntary? In order for the account of moral responsibility to have any plausibility at all, it seems, they must surely be voluntary. For suppose that they were not. Then an act of will would just be something that *happens* in me—like a chemical reaction or an elec-trical discharge—or happens *to* me—like a hypnotist's command. It would not be something in my control. Blaming *me* for my behavior under those circumstances would then make no more sense than blaming a bullet for exploding when struck by the firing pin. Something happened to it which caused it to explode. Similarly, if my acts of will were themselves involun-tary, something would have just happened to me which caused me to behave in a particular fashion. But it wouldn't be *my* fault.

So if the Volitionist theory is to supply an adequate account of the limits of moral responsibility, acts of will must themselves be voluntary. And in what will the voluntariness of an act of will consist? Why, in its having a special kind of cause, of course. An act of will is voluntary just in case it is caused by a volition, by *another* act of will.

And now we can see where the infinite regress comes in. For the same question—voluntary or involuntary?—arises for these new acts of will, and, for the same reasons, it must receive the same answer. It follows, then, that a voluntary act must be preceded by an infinite series of acts of will, each causing the act which follows it.

This discovery reveals an incoherence in the Volitionist theory. The theory holds, you will recall, that the voluntariness of an act consists in its being caused by an act of will. But what we have now discovered is that not just any act of will is good enough. It must, in fact, be a *voluntary* act of will. And if this is so, we haven't been given an answer to our original ques-tion. We can only understand *this* answer if we already know what makes an act of will voluntary. But our question is, What makes *any* act voluntary? The only course open to us is to apply the theory again. When we do so, however, all we find is that we need yet another *voluntary* act of will. The question does not go away.

That is the essence of the criticism. The question does not go away. That is what makes this challenge dialectical rather than logical. It disqualifies the proposed answer *as an answer,* for something qualifies as an answer to a question only if one can understand it without already knowing the answer to the question. The philosopher who offers this answer, therefore, violates a canon of rational practice. He commits himself to what is known in the trade as a *vicious* infinite regress. (An infinite regress which is not vicious, in contrast, is called *'benign'*.)

This, in outline, is the strategy of our third way to criticize a philosopher. The Volitionist theory of the voluntariness of acts fails, on this account, by having among its consequences a vicious infinite regress. It is an infinite *regress* because the voluntariness of an act will be secured only if the voluntariness of its volitional cause is already secured. The voluntariness of the cause must be accounted for *before* the voluntariness of the effect, if the cause itself is to guarantee the voluntariness of the effect. And it is a *vicious* regress because, given that the hypothesized volitional cause is itself an act (an act of will), the *problem* of supplying an account of its voluntariness is the same as the problem with which our inquiry began—the problem of accounting for the voluntariness of *any* act. The Volitionist proposal thus violates a canon of rational practice. It disqualifies itself as an answer to our original question, for something qualifies as such an answer only if one can understand it without already knowing the answer to the question.

Only an infinite regress which exhibits this sort of dialectical incoherence in a philosophical view is properly regarded as a *vicious* regress. And only the discovery of such a genuinely vicious regress carries indisputable critical weight. Determining whether a particular infinite regress is vicious or benign is a problem of the same delicacy and complexity as determining whether a given argument is or is not question begging. As with question begging, the dialectical environment of an infinite regress is crucial, for the same thesis may imply a benign regress in one setting, a vicious regress in another, and no regress at all in yet another. For these reasons, authentic cases of vicious infinite regress are relatively rare in philosophical practice—rarer, in fact, than many practicing philosophers think. Yet, as with genuinely question-begging arguments, occasionally the dialectical context is just right and an explanatory hypothesis is proposed which does imply a true vicious regress. If you can discover and exhibit such a case, then you will indeed have a third way to criticize a philosopher.

4. LOST CONTRAST

"Equality before the law" is a maxim which applies to the laws of logic more surely than to the laws of our imperfect society. As a positive principle, it requires that similar cases receive similar treatment. As a negative principle, it instructs us that unlike treatment of cases can be justified only if we can point to features exhibited by one case but not by the other. There is to be no discrimination unless there is a difference.

Applied to reasoning, the principle gives us yet another family of canons of rational practice. For arguments, it instructs us that like premises support like conclusions. For rational inquiry in general, it tells us that similar data confirm similar hypotheses and that analogous phenomena should receive analogous explanations. The underlying point of all these canons is this: The relations of support or implication between premises and conclusion, of explanation between theory and phenomenon, and of confirmation between data and hypothesis are all, in the broadest sense, logical relations—and logic is *formal*. The obtaining of logical relations is a matter of abstract patterns of reasoning and evidence rather than a matter of specific content. The similarities, likenesses, and analogies mentioned in the canons, then, are basically formal similarities. They concern the general pattern of premises, data, or phenomena without being overly worried about what those claims might say in detail.

Philosophers draw distinctions. The dialectical character of philosophical methodology regularly gives rise to *dichotomies*—divisions by pairs of concepts which are intended to *contrast* with one another, to exclude one another and stand in opposition. We have already played with a few of these and mentioned a few others—necessary versus contingent, free versus determined, mental versus material. One useful item to have in our critical toolbox, then, would be an instrument with which we could assess such distinctions or, more precisely, evaluate the reasoning with which some philosopher attempts to support one.

Our maxim of equality and the canons of rational practice to which it points are just such tools. Every distinction requires a difference. If there is no difference, the supposed distinction evaporates; the intended contrast is *lost*. What we need to do, then, is examine the sorts of considerations which a philosopher cites in favor of setting phenomena on one side or the other of a dichotomy. Suppose, for example, that a philosopher is trying to sort X's from Y's. Let us say that she classifies A as an X and B as a Y. Our maxim of equality tells us that this classification will be legitimate only if she can point to a relevant difference between A and B. If, on the other hand, for every consideration favoring classifying A as an X we can find a parallel consideration applying to B, and if for every consideration favoring classifying B as a Y we can find a similar consideration applying to A—if, in other words, we can show that there is no relevant difference between A and B—then the intended contrast is lost. A and B may both be X's or they may both be Y's, but if there is no difference, we may be sure, at least, that there can be no legitimate distinction in their classification. And now it's time for an example.

Perhaps the supreme master of this style of criticism was Bishop George Berkeley. The main distinction which Berkeley attempted to run to ground was that between *mind* and *matter*. There is nothing, he proposed to establish, which has an existence outside the mind. (On the face of it, this is a wholly outrageous thesis—but not when Berkeley gets finished with it!) The *esse* of the world is *percipi*—the existence of the world consists in its being perceived. To this end, Berkeley wrote for us three of the most charming dialogues in philosophy, the dialogues between Hylas (from the Greek *'hylē'*, meaning "matter") and Philonous (from *'philos nous'*, the "lover of mind"). These dialogues are gems of dialectic: Philonous inexorably presses the critical attack against a tenacious Hylas, who retreats slowly from formulation to reformulation but always holds fast to his root conviction that matter is *real*.

The question with which the first dialogue opens is whether *sensible qualities* exist outside the mind. By 'sensible qualities', Berkeley means those properties of objects accessible to the various senses—colors, shapes, sounds, flavors, odors, textures, and heat and cold. Hylas, of course, answers yes. Sensible qualities are "out there" in the world, in contrast, for example, with *pains,* which are merely "in us" and do not exist unless experienced (felt) by someone. Using the example of heat, Berkeley—speaking through Philonous—proceeds to criticize Hylas's distinction. He does so on the grounds of lost contrast:

PHILONOUS: Tell me whether, in two cases exactly alike, we ought not to make the same judgment?
HYLAS: We ought.
PHILONOUS: When a pin pricks your finger, does it not rend and divide the fibers of your flesh?
HYLAS: It does.
PHILONOUS: And when a coal burns your finger, does it any more?
HYLAS: It does not.
PHILONOUS: Since, therefore, you neither judge the sensation itself occasioned by the pin, nor anything like it to be in the pin, you should not, conformably to what you have now granted, judge the sensation occasioned by the fire, or anything like it, to be in the fire.[5]

Hylas would classify sensations of heat as "in the fire" but sensations of pain as "in us." Philonous replies that this is a distinction without a difference. Is the heat to be assigned to the fire because we feel it whenever the fire acts on us? Then the pain belongs in the pin, for we feel it whenever the pin pricks us. Is the pain to be assigned to us because it is a sensation which we feel? Then the heat is in us too, for it is also a sensation which we feel. For every consideration favoring classifying the heat as "in the fire" there is a parallel consideration applying to the pain, and for every consideration favoring classifying the pain as "in us" we can find a similar consideration applying to the heat. There is no relevant difference. The intended contrast is lost. Heat and pain may *both* be "out there," or they may *both* be "in us." This argument cannot, by itself, tell us which of those conclusions finally to endorse. But of this much, at least, we may be sure: There can be no distinction in their classification. A philosopher who, like Hylas, proposes unequal treatment for heat and pain without citing a relevant difference violates the

[5] George Berkeley, *Three Dialogues Between Hylas and Philonous* (Indianapolis and New York: Bobbs-Merrill, 1954), p. 18.

canons of rational practice. His supposed distinction rests on a lost contrast. And that is a fourth way to criticize a philosopher.

5. EMPTINESS

There is, I assure you, a demon in my wristwatch. How interesting, you may say. Let us open up the watch and have a look at it. You may open the watch, if you wish, I reply, but it will avail you little. I neglected to mention a salient fact: It is an invisible demon. Let me feel it, then, you say. Sorry, I answer, it's an intangible demon. Can I hear it? you ask. No, it's inaudible—and odorless and tasteless too, if it comes to that. Well then, you ask, how do you know it's there? Is it radioactive? No. Magnetic? No. Can you pick up its emanations on CB radio? No. Well then, you ask, does it at least affect the workings of the watch? Does the watch run slower or faster, for example, on account of the demon in it? I can save you a lot of trouble, I reply. It doesn't affect the workings of the watch at all. It is, in fact, a *wholly undetectable* demon. But, nevertheless, I assure you that there is a demon in my wristwatch.

And now, if you have your wits about you, what you say next is something like this: Tell me, what is the difference between a wristwatch containing a wholly undetectable demon and a wristwatch containing *no demon at all?*[6]

What shall we say about the claim "There is a demon in my wristwatch" in these circumstances? It is *true?* Well, suppose we say it is. What follows from that? It doesn't follow that anyone at any time in any situation will see or hear or smell or taste or feel anything in particular. It doesn't follow that the watch itself, or a Geiger counter, or a CB radio, or anything else, for that matter, will ever behave in any special way. Evidently, in fact, nothing at all follows from it.

Well then, shall we say that the claim is *false,* that there *isn't* a demon in my wristwatch? And what would follow from that? Just what would we be denying? What would we be ruling out? Why, exactly the same thing, of course—nothing at all. So it really doesn't make any difference what we say, does it?

At the beginning, it looked as if I were making a straightforward, although startling, claim about my wristwatch, rather like "There is a gear in my wristwatch" or "There is a mainspring in my wristwatch." (Both of which happen to be false, in fact—I have a solid-state digital quartz watch.) But now it turns out that I might as well have said, "There is a mulpsible in my

---

[6] This example is inspired by John Wisdom's "parable of the gardener," in *Logic and Language,* First Series, ed. Antony Flew (Oxford: Basil Blackwell, 1960), Essay X.

wristwatch" and, when asked what a mulpsible *is,* replied, "I haven't the foggiest idea."

For that matter, just what does my wristwatch have to do with what I said? If I had said, "There is a gear . . ." or "There is a mainspring . . . ," then by going on to say, "in my wristwatch," I would tell you *where to look* if you're interested in discovering whether what I said is true or false. But what's going on in my wristwatch turns out to be completely irrelevant to the question of whether "There is a demon in my wristwatch" is true or false. *Everything* turned out to be completely irrelevant to that question. You might as well look at my teacup or at your left shoe. Nothing you detected there would have any more bearing on the question than what you detect in my wristwatch. It seems that my claim wasn't really *about* my wristwatch at all. The words were there, all right, but for all the help they gave you in understanding what I was saying, they could just as well have been replaced by any other words.

For that matter, they could just as well have been replaced by no words at all. I might as well have said, "Astogobble mixplet is krand sumdickel." And would that be true or false? Why, it isn't even in the true-or-false line of work!

The amazing discovery is that the claim "There is a demon in my wristwatch"—although it *looked* quite different (and perhaps filled your imagination with many charming pictures)—turned out to be in the same boat. It isn't true and it isn't false either. It just isn't in that line of work. It's *empty*.

This is lost contrast, but with a vengeance—lost contrast carried to its final extreme. It isn't as if there were a perfectly good distinction between ordinary wristwatches and demon-inhabited wristwatches, the only problem being whether *your* watch and *my* watch should be classified the same way. We are worse off here than that. It's not that a distinction is being misapplied or applied groundlessly. Rather, no distinction has been established at all. The sentence "There is a demon in my wristwatch" hasn't been given any job to do. It has nothing to do with demons or with wristwatches or with anything else. It's just something I *say* from time to time, a noise that I make—but it's empty. A contrast has been lost, all right, but it's not the contrast between two sorts of wristwatches; it's the contrast between *saying something* and *just making noise*.

There's a canon of rational practice at stake here. One way to put it is this: Good grammar does not a thesis make. Meaningful claims must have meaningful consequences. Conversely, if, as the dialectic proceeds, a claim becomes progressively disconnected from all positive consequences, it loses its credentials as a *thesis* to be defended or criticized. To defend a claim is to argue for its truth; to criticize it is to produce reasons for its advocate to abandon it as false. Either procedure makes sense, however, only if it is presupposed that the claim is in the true-or-false line of work, that it is a claim with a content. For the acceptance or rejection of a thesis, you will recall, depends ultimately on whether it can successfully be shown to cohere or conflict with a large family of claims characteristic of a dialectical philosophical position. A claim totally disconnected from any positive consequences, however, can *neither* cohere *nor* conflict with any other claims. Such a claim, then, is neither defensible nor criticizable. It is not a *thesis* at all. It is empty.

And how does all this look in practice? A few pages ago, we met Hylas near the beginning of Berkeley's three dialogues. Look at him now, fighting and dying in the last ditch for the reality of matter:

PHILONOUS: . . . please . . . inform me after what manner you suppose [matter] to exist, or what you mean by its "existence"?

HYLAS: It neither thinks nor acts, neither perceives nor is perceived.

PHILONOUS: But what is there positive in your abstracted notion of its existence?

HYLAS: Upon a nice observation, I do not find I have any positive notion or meaning at all. I tell you again, I am not ashamed to own my ignorance. I know not what is meant by its existence or how it exists.

Philonous moves in for the kill:

PHILONOUS: When, therefore, you speak of the existence of matter, you have not any notion in your mind?

HYLAS: None at all.

PHILONOUS: Pray tell me if the case stands not thus: at first, from a belief of material substance, you would have it that the immediate objects existed without the mind; then, that they are archetypes; then, causes; next, instruments; then, occasions; lastly, *something in general,* which being interpreted proves *nothing.* So matter comes to nothing. What think you, Hylas, is not this a fair summary of your whole proceeding?

HYLAS: Be that as it will, yet I still insist upon it, that our not being able to conceive a thing is no argument against its existence.

PHILONOUS: That from a cause, effect, operation, sign, or other circumstance there may reasonably be inferred the existence of a thing not immediately perceived; and that it were absurd for any man to argue against the existence of that thing, from his having no direct and positive notion of it, I freely own. But where there is nothing of all this, where neither reason nor revelation induces us to believe the existence of a thing, where we have not even a relative notion of it, where an abstraction is made from perceiving and being perceived, from spirit and idea, lastly, where there is not so much as the most inadequate or faint idea pretended to, I will not, indeed, thence conclude against the reality of any notion or existence of anything; but my inference shall be that you mean nothing at all, that you employ words to no manner of purpose, without any design or signification whatsoever. And I leave it to you to consider how mere jargon should be treated.[7]

What Philonous is saying to Hylas (and thus, actually, what Berkeley is saying to his philosophical predecessor John Locke, who had advocated the reality of matter) is this: Your claim "Matter exists" is empty. By progressively insulating it from any positive consequences, you have emptied your claim of any content and reduced it to mere noise. And in so doing, you opt out of the game. I am relieved of my philosophical obligation to demonstrate an incoherence arising from your thesis for the simple reason that you are no longer advancing a thesis. "Where there are no ideas, there no repugnancy can be demonstrated between ideas." You have violated what is surely the most fundamental canon of rational practice, the basic presupposition of any method of rational inquiry—the requirement that there *be* a thesis into which to inquire. And so the game is over. Mind triumphs over matter, so to speak—but it wins by a forfeit.

And that, at last, is our fifth way to criticize a philosopher.

[7] Berkeley, *Three Dialogues,* pp. 67–68.

DEFINITIONS, ANALOGIES, AND THOUGHT EXPERIMENTS

Our judgment regarding the success or failure of a piece of philosophical reasoning is typically likely to hinge on the way in which we interpret or construe certain *terms* which play important roles in the dialectical proceedings. Sometimes these terms are bits of technical jargon—terms such as 'analytic', 'synthetic', 'a priori', 'a posteriori', 'counterfactual', 'substance', 'attribute', 'particular', and 'sense datum'—which philosophers have created or appropriated to signal certain ideas or mark certain distinctions which are less clearly delineated, or even not explicitly acknowledged, by our everyday vocabulary. Sometimes they will be terms drawn from that everyday vocabulary—terms such as 'certainty', 'necessity', 'idea', 'concept', 'sensation', 'rights', and 'values'—which, however, the philosopher is making especially precise in certain ways or putting to certain special uses in the service of his or her wider project. In any event, our judgment as to whether what a philosopher says is *true* will often turn on our understanding of what that philosopher *means* by what he or she says—and so it would be useful to explore briefly how you might go about *finding out* (or deciding) just what it *is* that some philosopher means.

It should also be noted that philosophers, alas, are not always so helpful as to present their views and reasonings in the form of direct arguments, needing only a bit of "tidying up" in order to identify their patterns, premisses, and presuppositions. Any philosophical work is, among other things, a *literary* entity, and its style can range from the dry formalism of a legal brief to charming dialogues of the sort which we have lately been examining. In addition to direct argument, then, you are likely to encounter in philosophical writings a rich set of *rhetorical* strategies, strategies aimed not so much at demonstrating a conclusion by logically deriving it from agreeable premises but at rendering a conclusion *plausible* by showing that it hangs together with other, well-understood, ways of thinking about the world, or that it could account for something which otherwise would remain puzzling and obscure. While there is, of course, no way to enumerate and examine all possible such rhetorical strategies, several are sufficiently frequent and fruitful to deserve mention in an introductory handbook such as this.

These, then, are the themes of the present chapter. I shall first say a few cautionary words about *meanings*—and, in particular, about "definitions" and dictionaries—and then discuss a pair of useful rhetorical strategies which are especially characteristic of philosophical writings—the use of *analogies* and the imaginative appeal to *thought experiments*.

WHAT YOUR DICTIONARY CAN'T TELL YOU

When you are puzzled by an unfamiliar word, the usual thing to do is to reach for the nearest dictionary—and what you find there is indeed often helpful. That is, what you find in a dictionary often serves to remove your initial puzzlement and to enable you to grasp what some author is driving at and get on with your reading. One common way of describing this sort of occurrence is in terms of "meanings." Initially, you are puzzled about "what the *author* means" because you don't understand "what some *word* means." You "look up the meaning of the word" in your dictionary, and, afterwards, you know both "what the word means" and "what the author means." Your puzzlement was a puzzlement about "meanings," and your appeal to the dictionary resolved that puzzlement. It is only natural, then, to suppose that what one finds in a dictionary *are* "the meanings of words," that a dictionary *contains meanings*. It is only natural—but it is also a mistake.

What one finds in a dictionary are not "the meanings of words" but *more words*. Indeed, that is the first rule of dictionary-making: Every word must have an *entry*, and every entry will consist of *other words*. A second rule is part of what makes the dictionary so helpful in cases like the one we've been describing: When the entry word is *unfamiliar* (rarely or infrequently used), the other words should be *more familiar* (commonly and frequently used). It would be a poor dictionary indeed which "defined" the entry word 'ambulatory' by offering 'peripatetic', when 'of or pertaining to walking' is ever so much more helpful.

Now *sometimes* it will, in fact, be the case that the other words following an entry word collectively do roughly the same job in speech and writing that the entry word itself does. Sometimes, that is, it would be in order to *replace* the entry word with the other words. Doing so would not materially distort the sense of the original text. In such a case, we can indeed speak of the dictionary entry as a "definition" and say that the other words are (roughly) *synonymous* with the entry word, that they "have (approximately) the same meaning." But it would be a mistake to conclude on that account that the dictionary "contains," or even "gives," meanings. What a dictionary contains is *more words,* and it "gives meanings" only in the sense that those other words are sometimes familiar and well-understood possible *substitutes* for the unfamiliar and puzzling entry words they stand alongside of.

Sometimes, however, the words standing alongside an entry word are not words which could *do* roughly the same job in speech and writing as the entry itself. Sometimes, for instance, they are words which *describe* that job or give *examples* of the entry word in action:

> **not:** used to express negation, denial, refusal, or prohibition: *It's not far from here. You must not do that.*

And sometimes the relationship between the other words and the entry word is fairly complicated:

> **green:** the color of growing foliage, between yellow and blue in the spectrum.

for instance, gives a pair of *recipes* for locating a *sample* of the color green: Look at some growing foliage, or look between yellow and blue in the spectrum. (Of course, you had better look at some *green* foliage. Some plants have *red* foliage, for example, and they'd be no help at all. And, by the way, do make sure that you've got a *complete* spectrum—and that you're not looking at it through a piece of colored glass.)

The editors of a dictionary arrive at their decisions regarding what to put next to an entry word in two ways. If the entry word is a common one, in widespread everyday use, they extract a large set of *samples* from novels, magazines, newspapers, transcripts of radio and television broadcasts, and other contexts in which the word appears and then attempt to diagnose from these samples the way or ways in which the word is *generally* used—the job or jobs it is usually doing in speech or writing—and to supply other words which either *do* roughly the same job or *describe* that job or are related to the entry word in some other potentially useful way (as in the example of 'green'). If, on the other hand, the word is unusual, rare, or technical—belonging, for instance, to the specialized vocabulary of medicine or biology or engineering or law . . . or philosophy—it will not be possible to assemble such a broad sampling of its use. In that case, the lexicographer relies upon a panel of *consultants* who are themselves academic *specialists*—physicians, biologists, engineers, lawyers, . . . or philosophers—seeking, and typically accepting, *their* recommendations for other words to put beside the unfamiliar entry word.

What follows from these facts of life, we can conclude, is that a dictionary is not a suitable place to look if your puzzlement about a word is a *philosophical* puzzlement, a puzzlement about the particular way in which some individual philosopher is using that word in a piece of reasoning which you are concerned to evaluate. If the term in question is a *familiar* one, being used in some limited, novel, or unfamiliar way in service of specific dialectical ends, then the dictionary's reconstruction of the usual and customary job done by that term in speech and writing is not likely to prove particularly helpful to you. But if the word in question is a *purely* technical term, then what the dictionary has to offer you is simply *another philosopher's conclusion* about what the first philosopher—the one you are reading—was up to, a conclusion which will inevitably be colored by the consultant's own philosophical views and characteristic vocabulary. In neither case, alas, will your dictionary "give you *the* meaning" of the troublesome term, much less "the *true* meaning."

For any such consultant specialist has arrived at his or her individual notion of what, for instance, Aristotle meant by 'form' and 'matter' in the *Metaphysics,* not by looking up 'form' and 'matter' in some dictionary, but by *studying the Metaphysics,* that is, by reading Aristotle's work and trying to puzzle out what Aristotle *meant by* 'form' and 'matter' from what Aristotle *said about* form and matter. And that, of course, is what you too will need to do in such cases—for, in the end, it is still your responsibility to decide whether or not such a consultant philosopher has understood Aristotle *correctly.*

At best, then, a dictionary's entries may serve to equip you with a *provisional* interpretation of some problematic terminology. Since dictionaries contain only humanly-formulated words and not divinely-inspired meanings, however, any such interpretation will at most be a point from which to begin. It will still remain for you to test that interpretation against the text itself—that is, to judge whether the philosopher's arguments indeed make sense when his vocabulary is understood in the suggested way and then, if they do, to judge whether, or that interpretation, they turn out to be compelling arguments. A dictionary is indeed useful—you should surely own a good one—but it cannot substitute for the hard work of philosophical thinking. For a dictionary can tell you neither what a word "*really* means" nor what some specific philosopher meant *by* that word (i.e., how he or she was individually using the word) on some particular dialectical occasion. It cannot tell you the former—the "real" or "true" meaning of a word—for there exists no such mythical beast to be hunted down. And it has no *special* authority with regard to the latter—a specific philosopher's particular usages— for, in the end, dictionary-makers have nothing to go on but what you yourself have to go on—the writings of that philosopher himself, and the fallible judgment of one or more human beings about how those writings are best and properly to be understood.

DIALECTICAL LIKENESSES

If someone finds it difficult to understand the structure of a hydrogen atom, it may be helpful to compare it to the structure of the solar system—the massive nucleus standing at the center like a sun and being orbited by a comparatively less massive "planetary" electron. If an anthropologist finds it difficult to describe the role of certain magical rituals in a primitive culture, she may find it useful to draw parallels between those rituals and certain religious rites found within her own culture. Analogical thinking, in other words, is a common tool for furthering understanding and communication in the physical and social sciences—and so too in philosophy. And this fact makes it appropriate to sound a cautionary note: Not everything which a philosopher says in the course of expounding and defending his or her point of view is intended to be (or should be) taken *literally*.

Sometimes, of course, the philosopher is quite explicit about his or her analogical intentions. In the *Republic,* for example, Plato turns from an investigation of the question "What constitutes a just *person?*"—that is, "What is the nature of this desirable trait of character, justice, in a virtuous individual?"—to consider the question "What constitutes a just *civil society?*"—that is, "What is the nature of this desirable condition, justice, in the Greek *polis* (city-state)?" His reason, he tells us, is that the *polis* is "the soul writ large." Not, of course, that the city-state *is* a giant soul, or the human soul a miniature city-state, but that there are important *analogies*—dialectical likenesses— between the individual soul and a political community, likenesses which can be exploited in a philosophical exploration of what contributes to the moral character of a virtuous person.

Such explicit analogizing is a perennial feature of philosophical thinking. We find it, for instance, in Locke's description of the human mind as a *"tabula rasa,"* a "blank tablet" upon which "experience writes its record." We find it in Rousseau's likening of the grounding of civil society to the signing of a "social contract" in which each participant agrees to surrender certain individual freedoms in the interest of a greater collective good. And we find it today, for example, in Thomas Kuhn's characterization of major theory changes in the physical sciences as "revolutions" and in the comparison of human cognitive processes to the workings of a digital computer, which has become a commonplace of contemporary philosophy of mind. In each case, the explicit intent is not to *identify* the one thing with the other, but rather to stress certain *similarities* of the one thing to the other—similarities the acknowledgment of which is seen as implying significant *philosophical* theses to be true of the subject of these analogical comparisons (for instance: that there is no "innate knowledge"; that the surrender of individual rights in a political community is not coercive; that "scientific progress" is partially determined by "irrational" socio-cultural factors; or that we need introduce no special "nonphysical" entities—a mind or a soul—to explain our own cognitive capabilities).

But analogical thinking also often plays a more subtle role in philosophical theorizing. Sometimes a certain dialectical similarity is not explicitly formulated in the interest of establishing a significant philosophical thesis but simply *taken for granted* in the *description* of some phenomenon which serves as the point of departure for further philosophical discussions. A philosopher engaged in offering a theory of sensations, for example, may proceed on the *assumption* that the sentence

(1)
Tom felt a sharp pain in his foot

is to be understood by analogy to

(2)
Ellen saw a red cup on the table.

The ensuing discussion is then likely to take some odd turns—turns which, in fact, are more or less "predetermined" by this tacit analogical presupposition. There will be worries about the "privacy" of pains. (Ellen and Eloise can obviously both see the *same* red cup. Can Tom and Timothy both feel the *same* sharp pain?) There will be worries about how one *counts* pains. (There's a difference between Ellen's seeing one red cup on two different occasions and her seeing two exactly similar red cups. Is there a difference between Tom's feeling one sharp pain twice and his feeling two exactly similar sharp pains?) And there will be worries about the locatability of pains. (If the table is in the kitchen, then when Ellen sees a cup on the table, she sees a cup in the kitchen. But even if Tom's foot is in his shoe, when Tom feels a pain in his foot, he does *not* feel a pain in his shoe. Why not?)

Whether an analogy be explicit or tacit, however, your approach to the critical appraisal of its cogency and pertinence remains the same. You need to ask, first, what *points* of analogy—what similarities or likenesses—the philosopher is proposing to exploit in his or her theorizing; second, whether those similarities or likenesses in fact *obtain;* and, third, whether there are any significant points of *dis*-analogy which vitiate the force of the intended or presupposed comparison. And it will often be useful in such cases to attempt to come up with a comparison of your own—an *alternative* analogy which highlights the *dis*-similarities between the two phenomena which the philosopher whose work you are evaluating is undertaking to assimilate to a single dialectical pattern.

You might, for example, engage Rousseau's explicit analogy between civic duties and contractual obligations on the issue of *voluntariness,* arguing that contracting parties commit themselves deliberately and self-consciously, whereas one is simply *born into* some civil society or other. And you might take on the tacit analogy between feeling a pain and seeing a cup by suggesting that the presumed *point* of the analogy—that "feeling," like "seeing," is a *relation* between a person and something else, some separate "object"—does not in fact obtain. Instead of understanding sentence (1) on the model of sentence (2), then, we might try to understand it by analogy with

> (3)
> Margaret wore a warm smile on her face,

and, noting that (3) is just a long-winded way of saying

> (3*)
> Margaret smiled warmly,

conclude that (1)—rather than pointing to a relation between Tom and some "private object"—is just a long-winded way of saying something like

> (1*)
> Tom's foot hurt sharply.

True prems
False conc.
Invalid
arg.

THE PLACE OF SCIENCE FICTION IN PHILOSOPHY

The final feature of philosophical writing I want to address in this chapter is philosophers' frequent employment of *thought-experiments*—that is, their imaginative description of situations which do not *in fact* obtain. Appeals to thought-experiments of this sort serve a variety of purposes in philosophical works, and, indeed, we have already encountered some of them in our discussions of validity and invalidity.

In using the method of modeling to demonstrate the invalidity of a form of argument, for example, we need to find an argument of the *same* form which has both true premises and a false conclusion. Now sometimes we are lucky. Sometimes we can just think of an argument which has the form we want whose premises *are* true and whose conclusion *is* false. But sometimes we are not so lucky—and, in such cases, a thought-experiment is precisely what we need. What we do is to imaginatively describe a situation which does *not* obtain, about which we can then construct an argument of the desired form whose premises *would be* true and whose conclusion *would be* false, if that situation *were* to obtain.

You may recall, for instance, my dog Spot (who would have four legs and a tail if he were a cat, and who *does* have four legs and a tail—but is *not* a cat). Well, the fact of the matter is that I don't have a dog named 'Spot'. I don't have any dog at all. The situation which I described in order to come up with some true premises ("If Spot is a cat, he has four legs and a tail" and "Spot has four legs and a tail") and a false conclusion ("Spot is a cat"), in other words, was a situation which does not in fact obtain. My counter-example was a thought-experiment. But it got the job done all the same. For, since an argument's form is valid only if its conclusion *must* be true when its premises are true, all that is required to show an argument to be invalid is a demonstration that it is *possible* for another argument to have both the same form and true premises, but for all that a *false* conclusion.

And this highlights, in fact, the characteristic role of such imaginative exercises in philosophical writing: The purpose of a thought-experiment is to demonstrate that something is *possible*. Now the sort of possibility which is typically of interest to philosophers is not practical or technological possibility (whether, for instance, it is now realistically practical or techno-logically possible to establish a colony on the moon), but rather what is called "logical possibility." A situation is *logically* possible just in case it can be described without logical absurdity, that is, without contradicting oneself. And philosophers are interested in logical possibility, in turn, because deter-mining whether some situation is logically possible is often a crucial step in determining whether *another* state of affairs is or is not *necessary* or in argu-ing that some problematic philosophical thesis is or is not in fact *true*.

Law enforcement agencies, for instance, use fingerprints to determine the identity of persons in their custody. If the fingerprints of a captured sus-pect match the fingerprints of a wanted criminal, the police and the courts regularly conclude that the suspect in custody *is* the wanted criminal. A philosopher interested in the question of what *necessarily* determines per-sonal identity, however, will point out that the principle "Sameness of finger-prints implies sameness of persons" is *not* a necessary truth, since we can easily imagine and describe a situation in which two persons are born with the same fingerprints or in which a clever surgeon perfects a technique for altering fingerprints. It is, in other words, *logically* possible for two persons to have identical fingerprints or for one person to have different fingerprints at different times (although, as far as we know, neither of these situations now *in fact* obtains).

Where such thought-experiments become particularly interesting is where the philosophical thesis at issue is a significant one and the situation being imaginatively described is correlatively complicated. A philosopher may attempt to convince us, for instance, that minds and bodies are *separate* entities by inviting us to imagine "two people *exchanging* bodies."

Surely you've ssen this depicted on television. Two people—Jack and Jill, let us say—sit in chairs to the left and right of an intricate electronic device. Metal helmets are lowered onto their heads. The infernal machine flashes and buzzes and hums and spits sparks. Jack and Jill slump forward unconscious. Finally, after a brief interval, the person who *looks* like Jack (call him 'John') stands up and claims to *be* Jill, and the person who *looks* like Jill (call her 'Judy') stands up and caims to *be* Jack. And what's more,

John now speaks and acts the way Jill used to speak and act, and Judy now similarly behaves the way Jack used to behave. This thought-experiment shows, our philosopher concludes, that it is *logically possible* for two people to exchange bodies. It follows that a person cannot be *identified* with a body, but must rather be a *mind*—something separate from any particular body which could, in principle, be *transferred* from one body to another.

The critical evaluation of philosophical conclusions grounded in such dramatic thought-experiments is a matter of some complexity. The most important point to keep in mind, however, is that what is at issue does not turn on anyone's powers of *imagination*. A state of affairs is logically possible, you should recall, just in case it can be consistently described, that is, described without contradiction or logical absurdity. Of course we can successfully imagine *something* in the case of Jack and Jill. What's crucial for our philosopher's conclusions, however, is how what we successfully imagine should correctly be *described*. What we need to look at, in other words, is what our philosopher *says* (or simply takes for granted) about what he asks us to visualize.

In this case, what is being claimed is clear enough. Our philosopher wants to say that, after the operation of the machine, John *is* Jill and Judy *is* Jack. And now you might ask: What criterion is being employed to *identify* Jack and Jill here? That is, how does one *determine,* after the experiment, who's who? It's clear enough that fingerprints, for example, *aren't* the criterion. But then, what is?

Well, it has to be John and Judy's *behavior,* doesn't it?—how they act and what they say about themselves. But now you can object that this only shows us who they *think* they are. A lunatic, for example, may *say* that he's Napoleon. He may even *act* like Napoleon. But that doesn't establish that he *is* Napoleon. And similarly, you can continue, John's claims and behavior don't establish that he *is* Jill (although he says he is), and Judy's don't establish that she *is* Jack (although she says she is).

You might criticize such a thought-experiment, in other words, by offering an *alternative description* of it. What we have imagined is not a machine for "putting Jack into Jill's body and Jill into Jack's body." What we have imagined is a machine for simultaneously inducing a particular kind of *insanity* (say, "acute delusionary personality psychosis") in two people—a machine which has driven both Jack and Jill mad, so that Jack now thinks he is Jill and Jill now thinks she is Jack.

Introducing such an alternative description "defuses" a thought-experiment, for it shows that the imaginative exercise with its vivid pictures does not support the intended philosophical conclusion (e.g., about minds and bodies) *by itself,* but only if one *takes for granted* certain additional premisses (e.g., about how to determine who's who)—premisses which you can then engage *argumentatively* in a critical discussion like that of any other, less picturesque, bit of philosophical writing.

SECOND
INTERMISSION

We have once again reached a point at which we would do well to pause and consolidate our gains.

What we have been discussing for the last three chapters is one basic form of philosophical essay, the critical examination of a view. There are other forms, of course, and I don't intend to neglect them, but the critical examination of a view is, in an important sense, the *fundamental* form, for it defines the sort of test which *any* philosophical effort must ultimately pass. A philosophical critique, so to speak, sets the boundaries of the playing field and lays down the basic ground rules of the game. Given the unavoidably systematic and dialectical nature of philosophical views, that is, the only measure which we can *ultimately* employ in evaluating the acceptability of any constructive *or critical* philosophical proposal—including your own!—is its ability to *stand up* under just this sort of critical examination.

In these chapters, we have spent considerable time probing the details of the notion of "internal incoherence" which lies at the heart of any dialectical critique. We have found it to range from the relatively straightforward, although rare, discovery of an explicit self-contradiction to the subtler, but correlatively more frequent, matter of violations of general "canons of rational practice." It is such violations which gave rise to what are characteristically thought of as particularly "philosophical" criticisms, and we have illustrated and explored five such criticisms in some detail—equivocation, question begging, infinite regress, lost contrast, and emptiness. While these are by no means the *only* ways in which a piece of philosophical reasoning can subtly take a wrong turn, like our more straightforward "froggy" invalid patterns of an earlier chapter, they are common enough confusions that you should be on the lookout for them—in your reading *and* in your own

writing—whenever an argument arrives at a conclusion which you have reason to suspect might not be entirely in order.

Extracting the argument from a philosophical text, we have noted, occasionally demands considerable exegetical skill, for philosophical essays are
also *literary* works in which unfamiliar words sometimes surface, familiar
words sometimes take on unfamiliar jobs, and rhetorical devices are pressed
into expository and argumentative service. While there is, in the end, no substitute for *practice* in mastering the art of coming to critical terms with a
piece of philosophical writing, I have tried, in the last chapter, to supply a
few tips, too, for dealing with questions of meaning when they arise in philosophical inquiry and for recognizing, appreciating, and even criticizing appeals to analogies and to thought-experiments in the conduct of a philosophical case.

All this has perhaps been rather a sizeable chunk of material to assimilate at one stretch, and, indeed, you are not likely to manage its assimilation
short of attempting yourself to *put it to use* in the writing of your own critical
examinations of some philosophers' arguments and views. Once you have
managed it, however, you will possess all the rudiments not only for understanding philosophical thinking as it is practiced by others, but for the
practical philosophical *exercise* of that understanding in your own thinking
and writing as well. What we need to do next, then, is to explore some of
the more elaborate discursive structures which may be developed from these
strategic themes—that is, some of the still larger patterns in which the critical
examination of a view may *itself* be embedded. Let me, therefore, bring this
second intermission to a close and raise the curtain on our next act, a discussion of some of the *other* species of philosophical essay which you are
likely to encounter in your reading—or be challenged yourself to produce in
your writing.

PHILOSOPHICAL ESSAYS

Adjudication of a Dispute

The most straightforward development of the critical examination of a view is the *adjudicatory* essay. Here the author acts as a third party to a philosophical dispute and attempts to arrive at an evaluation of the strengths and weaknesses of the competing positions. The adjudicatory essay may profitably be viewed as having a six-part structure:

1. Formulation of the issue
2. Exposition of position 1
3. Evaluation of position 1
4. Exposition of position 2
5. Evaluation of position 2
6. Resolution

There is nothing sacred about this ordering of elements, however. A student may often find it more convenient to proceed in the sequence 1–2–4–3–5–6, or to adopt an oscillatory "seesaw" strategy in the central portion of the essay, alternating between one position and the other until both have been exposed and explored piecemeal. Let me consider each of these six elements of an adjudicatory essay.

1. The formulation of the issue often makes severe demands on a student's interpretive abilities. Superficial peculiarities of terminology or expository style sometimes conceal disagreements or obscure potential agreement between the disputants, and a careful and thorough reading of both texts may be necessary to determine, from contextual clues provided by the detailed development of the argumentation, whether key terms are being understood and used in the same way by both parties. Again, as a result of

philosophy's dialectical methodology, the *visible* topics of discussion may be related only indirectly to the main underlying *issue* of contention. Recall that although the war is being waged over some central thesis, the battles may be fought at some distance, over supporting premisses. One useful strategy is to formulate the issue as a question to which the disputing parties do or would give differing answers. The question should be framed in such a way that it can be used as a guide to the reading of the disputing texts. Each text is then seen, through consideration of it in relation to that question, as argumentatively working toward some particular answer to it.

2 and 4. The task of exposition of the two positions, then, should be conducted through the medium of the issue under dispute as you have formulated it. The job becomes that of setting forth the structure of argumentation supporting each view on the disputed issue in such a way that the considerations offered by each disputant in support of his or her view can be seen to bear on that issue. Usually, this requires the student to *reconstruct* a piece of reasoning in reverse, so that the connections between the issue which is the philosophical starting point and the considerations which are the philosophical talking points can be clearly discerned. And this task is further complicated by the need to set out the two lines of reasoning in such a way that they make contact with *each other*.

3 and 5. This last remark also supplies a principal constraint on the project of evaluating the two positions. What the adjudicatory essay requires is that the adequacy of each of the two positions be evaluated from the standpoint of the *other* position. In the tidiest sort of case, one of the two texts will be a direct critical address to the views and arguments developed in the other text. In that case, the student will know what *one* of the two parties has to say about the considerations offered by his opponent in support of his views. But there remains the job of figuring out what that opponent *would* say in defense of his views and in reply to the criticisms offered by the first disputant. (Unfortunately, two philosophical texts cannot both be responses to each other.) This requires potential adjudicators to imaginatively place themselves in the shoes of that other philosopher, to imaginatively think themselves into the systematic viewpoint from which the text departs and attempt to use the resources of that viewpoint as the base from which to mount their critical assessment. And this demands a certain sympathy on the part of students. It demands that they read a text for its strengths as well as for its weaknesses, and that they allow each of the disputing parties his or her *strongest* possible case. Only in this way will the proposed resolution capture what is preservable about the two positions as well as what should be abandoned. Only in this way can progress be the clarification of authentic questions of substance rather than the knocking over of straw figures.

6. Only rarely will the final resolution amount to a judgment that one or the other of the disputing parties is wholly correct. More typically, what is called for is a careful interweaving of complementary insights, perhaps

supplemented by some of the student's own. A thorough critical exploration of competing positions often reveals that the initially formulated question has a complex underlying structure of presuppositions. It may unpack into a family of issues, some approached more fruitfully by one of the disputants and some by the other. Often, one needs most to construct and mobilize an assortment of distinctions—among different ways of reading some text, among different senses which can be assigned to some term, or among different interpretations which can be placed upon some fact, argument, or remark. And the noting of conceptual pitfalls—the marking of some false trails which have been or might naturally be pursued on some question—is frequently possible, even in the cases where no particular positive answer is clearly defensible, and is often no less useful than the obtaining of some positive result.

The well-turned adjudicatory essay, then, makes substantially greater demands on a student than the critical examination of a single view. Like a critical examination, the adjudicatory essay requires mastery of dialectical technique. But in addition, it requires students to attempt imaginatively to conduct at least one side of the discussion from a philosophical standpoint within which they do not feel at home. And this requires a standard of sympathetic exegesis and philosophical imagination higher than that typically evoked by the purely critical task. The adjudicatory essay, then, is one step on the road to lessening what often strikes students as the extreme negativity of the practice of philosophy, for it calls upon them to understand each of a pair of philosophical positions well enough to appreciate its strengths as well as its shortcomings. It calls upon them, if only for a moment, to become advocates of some view other than their own. When students begin to grasp the range of philosophical advocacies which are possible in this way, they have taken an essential step forward toward the coherent development of their own philosophical world views and toward becoming articulate and effective proponents of them.

PHILOSOPHICAL ESSAYS
Solving a Problem

Our third species of philosophical essay, like the second, is issue-oriented, but the solution of a problem draws more heavily on a student's originality and creative insight than on his or her exegetical and interpretive skills. Philosophical problems range from classical perplexities which have been unfolding over thousands of years of dialectical ramifications to brief set pieces constructed as exercises and illustrations. An essay devoted to one of the classical themes may nowadays be a fairly long book, whereas a classroom puzzle can often be dealt with in a couple of pages. In either case, however, there will be a discernible structure which, predictably, I shall now proceed to discuss.

Like the adjudicatory essay, the problem-solving essay may usefully be viewed as consisting of six parts:

1. Formulation and analysis of the problem
2. Development of criteria of adequacy for a solution
[3. Exploration of inadequate possible solutions]
4. Exposition of the proposed solution
5. Assessment of the adequacy of the proposed solution
[6. Replies to anticipated criticisms]

Again, you shouldn't regard this structural breakdown as somehow permanently chiseled in granite. Indeed, the brackets around 3 and 6 are intended to indicate that these are genuinely optional components. Also, what I have separated out as 1 and 2 will frequently be tangled together in a single passage or series of passages. And still other modifications are possible. But the six-part structure outlined above is a useful way to organize and think through a problem-solving essay, and, as a beginning student of philosophy, you would be well-advised to keep it in mind, at least until you develop some facility with the form.

Let me expand on this bare structural outline, not by providing an abstract discussion of each point, but by attempting to exhibit the scheme in action. Here is an example of the sort of compact problem which might be issued as a homework assignment for an introductory philosophy class. (I've actually used it in that way, and, truthfully, I hate to part with it. But it's in a good cause.):

Astronomers tell us that it takes four years for light to reach us from the nearest star. But during those four years, the star may have ceased to exist, and we can't see what doesn't exist. Do we ever see a star?

Let's work through this problem step by step according to the six-part scheme. What I'm going to do is to try to take it nice and slow so that you can follow, I hope, the process of thinking which leads up to such results as there are.

Before I begin, however, let me briefly address a question which perhaps occurred to you as you read the problem: Why bother? Who cares whether we ever see a star? I opened the book with some remarks about a sense of liberation and joy that can be reached through the practice of philosophy, you may recall. But what does *this* problem have to do with liberation and joy?

By itself, alas, not much. This handbook, after all, is concerned primarily with technique, and the sort of problem which is selected, for pedagogical reasons, as a good vehicle for illustrating certain points of technique is likely to be a rather unexciting one. The exciting ones are the complicated ones, you see, and the technical points tend to get lost among the complications. So there are, in fact, sound pedagogical grounds for selecting a "Who cares?" type of problem as an illustrative example.

But there's something else that needs to be said. Excitingness isn't a property of a thing like its color or size or shape. Whether or not something is exciting depends on what you can do with it, on how it connects up with other things that you care about. A footprint or fingerprint or cigarette butt isn't terribly interesting in its own right—but when it's a key clue that reveals the identity of a murderer, the discovery of a footprint or some such trivial thing can be very exciting indeed. Now if you're new to the philosophy game, you probably don't have very much to connect up with this little problem. It just sits there—a pointless exercise in a textbook. Well, I understand, and I sympathize with you. But there isn't very much I can do about that here.

Suppose, however, that you've embarked on the project of trying to get a comprehensive and coherent overview of the nature and limits of human knowledge—surely an exciting prospect. One of the main regions you'll need to map will be the territory marked "perception," a territory which encompasses seeing and hearing, feeling and smelling, and tasting. Many roads crisscross and wander through this terrain. Some are the rough, old, worn, dirt footpaths which I earlier called "common sense." Others, however, are new, clean, tidy, paved tracks laid down by the special sciences—neuroanatomy, physiological psychology, biophysics, and the like. Sometimes these roads cross harmoniously—there is an overpass or an underpass—or run along in parallel to one another. But sometimes they clash—and there is only an impasse. And when this happens, your effort to attain that joyful and liberating coherent understanding of human knowledge in general and perception less generally and seeing in particular is blocked. You have a problem to solve, a conceptual knot to untie, before you can get a picture that hangs together.

The little puzzle about seeing stars *can* be such a problem. And if you encounter it in that context, you will no longer be inclined to ask "Why bother?" For it will not then be an exercise but an *obstacle*—and the larger project which moves you, the goal of a coherent understanding which draws you onward, will supply all the reasons for bothering you could need or want.

This handbook cannot supply you with such a live context. No book can. Such things must arise from within you, from your own need or desire to understand something. The best I can do for you is to show you how to proceed, how such a conceptual knot might be unraveled. The most I can teach you is technique. The rest you must supply for yourself. And this takes time and it takes experience. Our projects are not given to us. We find ourselves with them; and we and they grow and mature together.

So much for apologetics. I shall do what I can do. Let me begin.

1. What *is* the problem here anyway? Well, there's an explicit question asked—"Do we ever see a star?" Is that the problem? It hardly seems likely. Of course we see stars, one is tempted to say. On any clear night we can see hundreds of them. That's just good common sense. What seems to be more problematic is the suggestion of an argument which looks like it's trying to establish that at least some of the times when we think we're seeing a star, we're actually *not*. Let's see if we can get the details of that argument out.

What's the relevance of the fact that light from stars takes years to reach us? Who cares about the light? Well, it hooks up with *seeing,* doesn't it? There's a bit of fairly simple-minded science being made use of here. I don't see something unless light from it enters my eyes and stimulates my retinas, triggering certain electrical events in my optic nerves and, ultimately, causing certain electrochemical changes in the visual cortex of my brain. So *if* we see a star, we don't see it until the light it emits arrives here and acts on us.

The next observation is that a star may have ceased to exist while it's light was on its way to us. Well, let's suppose that this happened; the star exploded or something. It's then supposed to follow that we *don't* see the star, because "we can't see what doesn't exist." Is that right?

Let's think about it for a minute. Often we distinguish between (really) seeing something and merely *seeming* to see it. One of the things that makes a difference here (although not the only thing) is whether or not the thing we think we're seeing actually exists. If it seemed to me that there was an oasis on the horizon or a colony of pink elephants in the corner and I later discover that there wasn't, I can't properly go on saying that I *saw* an oasis or some pink elephants. What I need to say is, "Well, I sure *thought* I saw an oasis (some pink elephants). I guess it was a mirage. (I guess I was hallucinating.)" It appears that we can't coherently both claim to really see something and grant that what we seem to see doesn't actually exist. The best we can do is something like this: "It's just *as if* I were seeing it." It seems fair to agree, then, that we can't see (really *see*) what doesn't exist. If what we think we're seeing doesn't exist, we don't actually see it. We only seem to see it.

But can we extract a problem from all this? I think we can. Let's start with the claim that we see stars all the time and know perfectly well that we do. We can assign that claim to the loose family of beliefs which I spoke of earlier as "common sense." It surely seems to belong there. Now, drawing on our bit of amateur science about stars and about seeing, we can construct two possible descriptions of what might be going on in the world on one of those occasions when we *think* we're seeing a star:

Case 1: Light emitted from a star some years ago acts on us and causes us to have the experience which we call "seeing a star." Nothing untoward has happened to the star. It's just where it seems to be.
Case 2: Light emitted from a star some years ago acts on us and causes us to have the experience which we call "seeing a star." However, sometime during the intervening years the star has exploded, and now it no longer exists. There is now actually nothing where there seems to us to be a star.

In case 1, we do see a star. But in case 2, since we can't see what doesn't exist, we don't see a star. The problem is this: We can't tell whether a particular experience of seeming to see a star is an example of case 1 or case 2. How could we? What happens to us (to our retinas, our optic nerves, and so forth)—and the experience we have because of it—is the same in both cases. So it might be the case that all instances of seeming to see a star are of the case 2 kind. And, if so, we never would see a star.

The underlying problem, then, is an apparent clash between common sense and science. Although it's been very crudely drawn, the conflict goes roughly like this: Common sense proposes that we know perfectly well that we sometimes see stars, but scientific inquiry has uncovered a bunch of facts about stars and about seeing which seem to imply that we, in fact, can't know whether we ever see stars or not. The question we need to address is how this apparent conflict is to be resolved.

2. Well, what's wanted of a solution? What would we like to be able to accomplish? The nicest thing would be to save both our amateur science and our unsophisticated common sense. In any case, we're not going to quarrel with the science. If some physiologist claims that light must impinge on the retina before a person can see, for example, we have no grounds on which to quarrel with her. We lack the relevant professional expertise. So one condition of adequacy we might lay down for a solution is that it recognize that stars are trillions of miles away, that light takes years to travel from them to us, that we see a star, *if* at all, only when light emitted from it has acted on us, and so on. But let's see if we can salvage the little piece of common sense, too. It would be nice if it turned out that we often do see stars and know perfectly well that we do. So let's try requiring that any adequate solution save that claim, too, that it accept the claims we're calling "common sense" as well as the claims we're calling "science." There's no guarantee that a solution to the puzzle which does endorse all of these claims exists, of course, but it's worth a try.

3. If we've adopted these restrictions on a solution to the puzzle, there's one very tempting proposal which we can dismiss right away. This is the proposal that we *don't* really see stars; what we really see is the *light* emitted by the stars. This saves our science, all right, but it does so at the price of our common sense. And we've decided to try not to do that. In fact, there are lots of other good reasons for not succumbing to this tempting proposal. Having a look at them might give us a clue as to how we might solve our original problem.

For one thing, if we never see stars but only the light they emit, then we never see anything but light—emitted light or reflected light. Now this might seem all right, until we began to reflect on the reasons people could have for believing those claims we've been calling the claims of science, including the claim that we don't see anything unless and until the light which it emits or reflects acts on us. Presumably one finds this out by making observations. But if we don't see anything but light, then we don't see the meters, dials, telescopes, microscopes, mirrors, lenses, and other apparatus which we surely need to make those observations. So the very facts which supposedly imply that we don't see anything but light appear to be facts that we couldn't *know* if it were true that we didn't see anything but light.

In fact, the view that what we actually see is light, we might argue, really rests on a straightforward confusion—a confusion between *what* we see and *how* we see it. Let's grant that we don't see anything until the light it emits or reflects acts on us. That only tells us how we see something: We see it by means of the light it emits or reflects. What we see, however, is the object that emits or reflects the light. The light is the medium of sight, not the object of sight.

If we accepted the view that we see only light, we might as well hold instead that we see only our own eyes. For, after all, we don't see anything unless and until our eyes are stimulated—and "like premisses support like conclusions." But again, what we should say is that that's *how* we see something, not *what* we see. The eyes are the organs of sight, not its objects.

So this tempting proposal is one that we should pass by. But it gives us a clue to philosophical methodology, for it suggests that what may be called for is the careful drawing of a distinction, like the one between what we see and how we see it. Perhaps there's some other distinction which we've been overlooking.

4. From the original formulation of the problem, recall, I extracted or constructed (depending upon how imaginative you thought I was) a little argument. What we need to do is to get inside that argument. In particular, let's take a more careful look at the key extra premiss: "We can't see what doesn't exist." Earlier, I gave a brief defense of this principle by pointing out the common-sense distinction between seeing something and merely seeming to see something. The examples I appealed to were mirages and hallucinations. But now, thinking in terms of drawing distinctions, it may occur to you to look for some way in which these cases are importantly *different* from the case of an exploded star. ("No distinction without a difference.") Once you put the question that way, it almost answers itself. In the case of a mirage, there *never is* an oasis at that spot in the desert, and in the case of a hallucination, there *never is* a colony of pink elephants in the corner. But in the case of an exploded star, there *once was* a star in that region of space. It's just that there isn't one there now. So we might distinguish what never exists (what doesn't exist at all) from what doesn't exist now, at the time we're having our experience.

This gives us two readings for our key premiss: "We can't see what doesn't exist." We could read it as "We can't see what doesn't exist at the time we seem to see it," or we could read it as "We can't see what *never* exists." But which reading is at work in our argument? The answer seems to be: "Both!" For it's the first reading that I needed in case 2 in order to conclude that we don't see a star, but it's the second reading which I defended by citing mirages and hallucinations and by contrasting actually seeing with merely seeming to see. There are some reasons for accepting the premiss as true according to the second reading, then, but we've been given *no reason at all* to accept it if we interpret it according to the first reading. And this gives us a way to solve the original problem.

5. What we wanted to do was to preserve our common-sense belief that we often see stars and know perfectly well that we do without challenging any of the results of physical science. And we are now in a position

to do this, provided that we have a sufficiently refined understanding of our extra premiss. Return again to our two cases. The problem, you will recall, was generated by three conclusions: (1) in case 1 we do see a star; (2) in case 2 we don't see a star; and (3) we can't tell the cases apart. But we can now see that there is a way open to reject the argument which led us to the second of these conclusions. We argued for conclusion 2 on the ground that we can't see what doesn't exist. That conclusion follows, however, only if we interpret that premiss in the first way: We can't see what doesn't exist at the time of our experience. And we are free to reject that interpretation. Consideration of examples of merely seeming to see—hallucinations and mirages—gave us reasons to accept only the second interpretation: We can't see what never exists. But according to that interpretation, we no longer have any reason for concluding that case 2 isn't a case of seeing a star. The premiss no longer supports that conclusion. We can consistently hold that both in case 1 and in case 2 we *do* see a star, and no conflict remains to plague us.

6. It may be objected that this solution doesn't provide us with any way of telling whether any particular experience of seeming to see a star is of the case-1 kind or of the case-2 kind. And this is correct. But it is not an objection. Our inability to distinguish between the two kinds of cases was a *problem* only because we thought that the difference between the cases was the difference between seeing and not seeing a star. Since we now understand that we need not be committed to that conclusion, we may contentedly reply that telling about a particular case always requires particular investigation. Of course it does. In this instance, the procedure is a straightforward one: We just wait the appropriate number of years. If the star has exploded in the meanwhile, we'll get a look at the explosion sooner or later. There's no reason to suppose that we should be able to tell whether we're in case 1 or case 2 *just* by examining the single experience we're having at the time. That's neither "common sense" nor science. In fact, the same is true of experiences of seeing, as opposed to mirages or hallucinations. We can't tell by examining the *single* experience we're having that there isn't an oasis at that spot or a colony of pink elephants in the corner. We have to go and check it out.

But it might be objected that it's still possible that *all* the cases in which we think we're seeing a star are of the case-2 kind—or, worse, that in all the cases in which we think we see *anything*, what's really going on is that we're hallucinating. Well, this gets us into deeper dialectical waters, but I can make two brief remarks which defuse the immediate objection. On the one hand, it might indeed be the case that all the stars we will be seeing tonight exploded simultaneously about two years ago. No amount of pure armchair reasoning can somehow guarantee that it didn't happen. In that event, we'd be in case 2 with a vengeance. In fact, I would suppose that astronomers have some good reasons for believing that it's extremely unlikely that any such thing happened. But so what? Even if it has happened, we don't need to give up any of the scientific or common-sense claims at issue. For we understand now that we can consistently hold that case 2 experiences are examples of seeing stars. (Of course, the *non*philosophical consequences of such a stellar explosion remain a matter of legitimate concern.)

And as for that more troublesome possibility—well, how does the reasoning go? It looks to me as if it consists of two steps:

(A)   We can't tell by examining a single experience we're having
                 that it's not a hallucination.
             _____
             So, any experience could be a hallucination.

(B)   Any experience could be a hallucination.
             _____
             So, it could be the case that all experiences are hallucinations.

And, if this *is* how the reasoning goes, we're in no trouble. *A* may or may not be okay, but if you think about *B* for a minute, you'll discover that you already know what to say about it.

This concludes my illustration and discussion of the problem-solving essay. There are a few specific observations which you should carry away with you. Probably the most important of these is how much of the work consists in getting clear about just what the problem *is*. That's by far the largest of the six parts in my example, and this isn't extraordinary. It's typical. Only when we reconstructed the set problem as a conflict of arguments based in science and in common sense could we see where conceptual pressure needed to be brought to bear. And we also needed the detailed analysis of the problem to suggest criteria of adequacy sufficient to steer us away from the tempting, but ultimately confused, proposal that we really see only light. Time spent in spelling out a problem, in laying bare and making fully articulate the presuppositions and principles underlying the set question, is time well spent. It is better to invest your energies in such a detailed formulation and analysis than to batter yourself to pieces on the rocks of a problem for lack of a genuine understanding of what the problem is.

It is worth noting, too, how easily a minor philosophical set piece of this sort opens out into the much larger questions of the reliability of sensory perception in general and the relative authoritativeness of common sense and empirical science viewed as codifications of what we properly know. This is a further reflection of the systematic and dialectical character of philosophical viewpoints on which I remarked earlier. Any philosophical picture is, at least implicitly, a total world view, and a tug on any dangling thread vibrates the whole web.

PHILOSOPHICAL ESSAYS
Defense of an Original Thesis

It is unlikely that you will be called upon as a student to articulate and defend a wholly novel philosophical conception. And this is for the best. Unlike our earlier forms, the defense of an original thesis resists being captured in a recipe. Of course any such defense must contain an exposition of the proposed thesis or view, together with the development of a set of considerations in support of it. Frequently, the author of such a defense will also wish to anticipate and meet certain natural criticisms of the view, ward off certain potential misunderstandings, or elaborate upon the philosophical consequences—perhaps even upon the practical consequences—of adopting it. Not infrequently, however, such an original world view includes a profoundly new methodological conception, a new metaphilosophy, which itself constrains the form of philosophical exposition. Moreover, a philosophical thesis which is radically creative may place severe demands upon the literary talents of its proponents. For such reasons, the influential major writings of the great philosophers are often moving literary works of extraordinary grace and power. They range in expository form from the spirited dialogues of Plato's Athenians to the crystalline geometry of Spinoza's *Ethics,* from the powerful mythic aphorisms of Nietzsche's *Zarathustra* to the seemingly loose collection of suggestive, superficially unrelated, numbered paragraphs assembled by Wittgenstein as his *Philosophical Investigations.* When we turn from critique, adjudication, and problem solving to the theme of creativity in philosophy, we pass, as we do in *any* discipline, beyond the point at which our subject is teachable. I cannot give guidance as to how to write such works. The most I can do is suggest some strategies for reading them. It is to this final topic which I now turn.

SIX WAYS TO READ A PHILOSOPHER

Philosophical writings are not for reading through; they are for reading down into. That is why the contents of philosophy courses—unlike the contents of say, mathematics or biology courses—are not stratified by difficulty or complexity. In mathematics, one masters multiplication and division before geometry and algebra, geometry and algebra before trigonometry and calculus. In biology, one dissects an earthworm before a frog, a frog before a mouse. But in philosophy, one learns to crawl, to walk, and to run over the same landscape. In philosophy, one begins where one ends—with Plato and Aristotle, with Descartes and Hume—indeed, with the whole galaxy of great philosophers, their writings, and their concerns. What varies through one's development as a student of philosophy is not the objects of one's encounters but the form and depth of one's encounters. The writings of a philosopher can thus be read in many ways. Here are six:

1. YOU CAN READ A PHILOSOPHER FOR CONCLUSIONS *What*

This is perhaps the most common first-time approach for the beginning student or philosophical layman. You read a person's work to find out *what* he or she thinks. You assemble a list of views and opinions. If investigation ends here, what comes out is the taxonomic (labeling) style of studying philosophy. One assigns everybody to the appropriate "isms"—realism, idealism, empiricism, rationalism, existentialism, utilitarianism, intuitionism, logicism, nominalism, and so on. The possibilities for classification and subclassification are endless. There is some point to getting a handle on these groupings.

It gives one a rough overall map of the philosophical terrain. For someone who is interested in a piece of philosophical writing mainly as a cultural or historical artifact, as an episode in the history of ideas, this approach may well suffice. But for a student of philosophy, it's only the beginning.

2. YOU CAN READ A PHILOSOPHER FOR ARGUMENTS   *Why*

Probably the next step is to attempt to press beyond the content of the conclusions, the theses and views which a philosopher accepts, to an appreciation of the structure of reasoning underlying and supporting them. Here you read a person's work to find out not just what he or she thinks, but *why* he or she thinks it. One beneficial by-product of this approach is the insights it yields concerning the connections among a philosopher's views, the ways in which the various conclusions hang together or fail to hang together, support or undermine one another. A careful reading of a philosopher in this way, for the purpose of exposing and articulating the structure of the reasoning, is an essential foundation for any further approach to philosophical works. But it is a foundation which can be built upon in various ways.

3. YOU CAN READ A PHILOSOPHER IN THE DIALECTICAL SETTING   *How*

Every philosopher enters our great historical conversation at some specific time. Every philosopher has predecessors and teachers, colleagues and opponents. The discussion, the meeting of arguments with arguments, is already well under way. One thing you can do with the raw materials obtained from your reading for conclusions and for arguments is to attempt to sort out the dialectical contribution which a philosopher proposes to make. How have the central concerns and problems of the discussion been conceived, and what new way are we given for looking at them? What new questions are asked? What false trails are marked and blocked? A major work by a great philosopher is a stone dropped into a pool of concepts and problems. To read a philosopher in the dialectical setting is to examine the ripples that such a splash creates, and to mark the ways in which they cancel and reinforce the many other sets of ripples stirring the surface of the pool. A philosophical problem is changed by the touch of a great mind. What it was before, and what it has become, are the concerns of our third style of reading. If reading for conclusions is reading for what a person thinks, and if reading for arguments is reading for why he or she thinks it, then reading in a dialectical setting is reading for *how* that person thinks—and this is the most difficult of the three tasks.

But so far we have called only upon the reader's exegetical and interpretive skills—the ability to think oneself into a philosophical view, to understand it, to reconstruct the reasoning supporting it, and to discern its implications in its dialectical setting. As in the writing of philosophy, however, there is scope for more than exegesis and interpretation.

4. YOU CAN READ A PHILOSOPHER CRITICALLY

The conclusions are there. The arguments are there. Once you understand them, then, you can proceed to assess them. This is the critical reading of philosophy. To do it, you need to enter into a dialogue with the book. To each of a philosopher's positive views or claims you can set the critical questions: Is it true? Does it follow? The answers which you come up with, however, are more than a test of the philosophical viewpoint at issue. Significantly, they put your understanding of that viewpoint to the test. For you need to appreciate more than what the philosopher says and why he or she says it. You need to have a grasp, too, of what the philosopher *would* say in response to your exploratory probes and critical thrusts. Only when you achieve this sort of imaginative and sympathetic understanding of a philosophical stance can the critical attitude yield more than superficial quibbles. Only then can your critique bear importantly on what is essential to the view. So you need to understand not just what and why and how a philosopher thinks. To read critically, you must also discern, what *turns* on the view at hand. And, of course, you will not be the first to try. So,

5. YOU CAN READ A PHILOSOPHER ADJUDICATIVELY

To approach philosophy in this fifth way is to multiply immensely the demands placed upon your analytical skill, extrapolative insight, and critical acumen. An adjudicative reading approaches a philosophical work in its dialectical setting as a critical reading approaches it in isolation. The aim here is not merely to appreciate the novel turns which a philosopher has given an old problem, but to attempt to gauge the import of the contribution, to assess the philosopher's understanding and criticism of his or her predecessors and contemporaries, and to evaluate the fruitfulness of the new questions and methods, and of the new directions they give to philosophical inquiry. To accomplish this requires something quite like a carefully controlled schizophrenia, for you must move sympathetically within a diversity of philosophical viewpoints—often developed through strikingly different expository idioms and embodying radically divergent conceptions of philosophical methodology. You must attempt imaginatively to take the role of each of the original participants and to rethink the dialectic in its entirety from *all* these viewpoints. For what is wanted is more than an appreciation of the new insights to be gained. No less important is that old insights not be permanently lost. The adjudicative reader thus cannot approach the dialectic as a partisan, for the concern is with the isolation and preservation of all that is of lasting philosophical value. And this sets the stage for our final possibility.

6. YOU CAN READ A PHILOSOPHER CREATIVELY

When you can approach a philosophical work in this sixth way, you will have crossed a major conceptual watershed. You will have made its author's problems your own. No longer will you engage a piece of philosophical writing as an academic exercise. You will be on a quest. There will be something about people and their relations to the universe which you need to understand, some conceptual tangle which resists your unraveling. When you turn to the great philosophical figures of the past, then, it is with the aim of exploring a wider range of conceptual options than you are capable of evolving on your own, and it is with the goal and hope of eventually finding a way to your own resolution of the puzzles that haunt you. More than this, however, cannot easily be said. For creative reading of philosophy resists codification no less than creative authorship. And so I have again reached the limits of what is teachable.

RETROSPECT

A handbook of this sort can have only limited value. Philosophy is a practice, and its mastery is the mastery of a cognitive skill, not the assimilation of a body of facts. The practicing philosopher is a conceptual craftsman. Ultimately, then, philosophy, like any other craftsmanly pursuit, can be mastered only through the doing of it. The beginnings of such mastery evolve only gradually out of a long series of failed attempts. Behind every masterwork of cabinetry lies an ancestry of wobbly bookcases and skewed sideboards. So it is, too, with philosophy.

A few hours before his death, Socrates offered some reflections on pain and pleasure.

> What a queer thing it is, my friends, this sensation which is popularly called pleasure. It is remarkable how closely it is connected with its conventional opposite, pain. They will never come to a man both at once, but if you pursue one of them and catch it, you are nearly always compelled to have the other as well; they are like two bodies attached to the same head. I am sure that if Aesop had thought of it he would have made up a fable about them, something like this: God wanted to stop their continual quarrelling, and when he found that it was impossible, he fastened their heads together; so wherever one of them appears, the other is sure to follow after. That is exactly what seems to be happening to me. I had a pain in my leg from the fetter, and now I feel the pleasure coming that follows it.[1]

The frustration of bondage is not merely a prelude to the joy of release. Paradoxically, it is its indispensable precondition as well. Philosophy is that way too, of course. Sadly, beginning students in philosophy live more with philos-

[1] Plato, *Phaedo*, trans. F. J. Church (Indianapolis and New York: Bobbs-Merrill, 1951), p. 4.

ophy's agony than with its ecstasy. And this is unavoidable. But it is worth staying with it. For, unlike release from the bondage of fetters, breaking through the encrustations of frustrated thought to a clear and coherent philosophical overview of some complex conceptual terrain is a distinctively *human* pleasure, available only to us animals whose life is a life of speech and reason. One cannot experience it without being changed. What you discover is the true locus of relevance. The unrestrained activity of reason, in the end, is what is *most* relevant to us as we are, for we are reasoning animals. And to grasp that truth is to make a part of you the conviction by which Socrates lived and for which he died: that the unexamined life is not worth living.

APPENDIX

PUZZLES

1. It is sometimes said that space is empty, which means presumably, that there is nothing between two stars. But if there is *nothing* between two stars, then they are not separated by anything, and, thus, they must be right up against one another, perhaps forming some peculiar sort of double star. We know this not to be the case, of course, so it follows that space isn't empty after all.

2. It has been suggested that one reason why cattle are so timid is that their eyes are so constituted that they see human beings and other animals much larger than they really are. Does this seem likely to you?

3. Descartes writes that "stars or bodies at a great distance appear to us much smaller than they are." How near would we have to be to stars in order for them to appear the right size (that is, the size that they actually are)?

4. Could a person who was blind from birth know what the word 'red' means? By the way, what does the word 'red' mean?

5. When it's 12:30 P.M. in Newark, what time is it on Neptune?

6. When a straight swizzle stick is placed in a glass containing a whiskey and soda, we observe that it looks bent. If we investigate further, we may discover that it feels straight. What we usually go on to conclude is that it looks different from what it is, although it still feels the way it is. But that's silly. There's no good reason for not concluding instead that the stick is (now) bent. It only feels straight, but the way it looks is the way it is. It's the way that it feels that is now different from what it is. Is that right?

7. "John Doe may be a relative, a friend, an enemy, or a stranger to Richard Roe, but he cannot be any of these things to the Average Taxpayer. He knows how to talk sense in certain sorts of discussions about the Average Taxpayer, but he is baffled to say why he could not come across him in the street as he can come across Richard Roe."

Both Richard Roe and the Average Taxpayer may be male, thirty-four years of age, married, homeowners, and earning $9,500 per year. But Richard Roe can live in Davenport, Iowa, have a wife named 'Amy', drive a Buick, and have maple trees growing in his front yard—and the Average Taxpayer can't. Of course, the Average Taxpayer can have 2.6 children and own 1.3 automobiles—and Richard Roe can't. How do you explain all this?

8. Dogs can hear sounds that are too high for people to hear. Could there be sounds too high for *any* animal to hear?

9. The Greek Sophist Protagoras was so convinced of his effectiveness as a teacher of law that he once trained a pupil at no charge, on the condition that the student would pay his fee from the proceeds of the first court case the student won. After he was trained, however, the pupil refused to begin legal practice, so Protagoras sued to recover his fee. In court, Protagoras argued that, win or lose, the student must pay—by the terms of their agreement if the student won the case, and by the verdict of the court if the student lost it. The clever pupil, however, replied that the payment was forfeit in either case—by the terms of their agreement if he lost the case, and by the verdict of the court if he won it. Does Protagoras get his fee or not?

10. Suppose Achilles runs ten times as fast as the tortoise and gives the creature a hundred yards' start. In order to win the race, Achilles must first make up for his initial handicap by running a hundred yards. But when he has done this and has reached the point where the tortoise started, the animal has had time to advance ten yards. While Achilles runs these ten yards, the tortoise moves one yard ahead; when Achilles has run this yard, the tortoise is a tenth of a yard ahead; and so on without end. Achilles never catches the tortoise, because the tortoise always holds a lead, however small.

11. "If my mental processes are determined wholly by the motions of atoms in my brain, I have no reason to suppose that my beliefs are true. Hence, I have no reason for supposing my brain to be composed of atoms."

12. If you see some part of an apple but not every part of the apple, then you see not an apple but only part of an apple. Since no one ever sees every part of an apple, no one ever sees an apple. The argument isn't restricted to apples. Peaches, pears, plums, cars, books, and people—no one ever sees them. Indeed, no one ever sees anything. What's gone wrong here?

13. Giving a poor man a penny does not alter the fact of his poverty: If he was poor before you gave him a penny, he's poor after you gave him the penny. A man with one penny to his name is certainly poor. Give a poor

man a penny and he's still poor. So, a man with two pennies is poor. The same with three pennies. And four pennies. But if one keeps on long enough, the fellow has billions and billions of dollars. And a man with billions and billions of dollars certainly isn't poor. Sure, something's gone wrong with our reasoning here—but where and what?

14. "Since there is only one God to worship, a person who worships a God cannot but worship the true God." Then what is all the fuss about?

15. "If you don't believe that there is a God who created and designed the universe, then you must believe that everything that happens and that ever has happened is one vast *accident*." Is that right?

16. What I see depends upon the state of my sense organs. Physical objects do not depend upon the state of my sense organs. Therefore, I do not see physical objects.

17. The way we assess any rule of inference which is questioned is to examine a sample of inferences drawn in accordance with the rule and observe whether or not the rule has been successful. If in almost all cases the inference proved to be correct, we may properly argue that the rule of inference has been justified. Now the following rule has been used in a wide variety of cases and has proved highly successful:

> **R:**
> *From* "All hitherto observed A's have been B's"
> *Infer* "A's observed henceforth will probably also be B's"

Therefore, we may conclude that it will probably continue to be successful in the future, and we are justified in continuing to use it.

18. A benevolent being would eliminate evil and suffering if he could and if he knew about them. An omniscient being would know about any evil or suffering, and, of course, an omnipotent being could eliminate evil and suffering if he wanted to. But God is supposed to be omniscient, omnipotent, and benevolent. Why, then, is there evil and suffering in the world?

19. No matter how good a universe God in fact created, he could always have created a better one, for there is no such thing as the best possible universe, just as there is no such thing as the highest possible integer. It follows that we can make no moral criticism of God, since there is nothing that we can blame him for having failed to do. Is this right?

20. Just as a dissonant chord can contribute to the overall beauty of a symphony, and just as ugly brushwork can contribute to the total aesthetic effect of a painting, so it may be that evil and suffering are necessary components for the best of all possible worlds. If so, then we cannot morally censure God for permitting them. Is this right?

21. Could two objects differ *only* in length?

22. We're all taught in elementary school that we can't add apples and oranges. We're also taught that we *can* add apples and apples. "2 apples + 2 apples = 4 apples" is supposed to be true. Well, you probably know how to peel or eat or throw apples. But just how does one *add* apples?

23. Either God exists or he doesn't. Neither claim can be proved true. Thus, we must wager. If we wager that God exists, and we are right, we win everything; if we are wrong, we lose nothing. If we wager that God doesn't exist, and we are wrong, we lose everything; if we are right, we win nothing but we also lose nothing. This is clearly the opportunity of a lifetime. Any reasonably prudent person should be eager to bet that God exists, and thus to lead the life of a believer.

24. One Friday, a professor announced to her class that on one of their five meeting days during the next week, she would administer to them a *surprise quiz*. The class would not know which of the five days it would take place until the morning on which it was actually to be given. One of her students argued as follows: "You cannot give the quiz on Friday, for if it had not taken place on one of the four earlier days, we would know on Thursday night that it was to be given on Friday and it would not be a surprise. Similarly, it cannot be given on Thursday. Friday is out, so if it had not been given on one of the first three days, we would know on Wednesday night that it was due on Thursday. Again, it would not be a surprise. Obviously, the same sort of argument applies to Wednesday, Tuesday, and Monday. It follows that you cannot give a surprise quiz at all." The professor was puzzled. She had decided to give the quiz on Wednesday, and she was quite sure that the students didn't know that. But she found the student's argument convincing, so she canceled the quiz. Should she have?

25. Does the box below contain a true sentence or a false sentence?

> The sentence in the box
> on page 102 of *The Practice
> of Philosophy* is false.

26. If there are no such things as Santa Claus and the Tooth Fairy, then what are you talking about when you explain to a child that there are no such things as Santa Claus and the Tooth Fairy?

27. Sometimes we think about the moon. What makes thinking about the moon thinking about the moon, and not thinking about anything else?

28. Suppose that, in fact, no great person has ever been born in the Aleutian Islands. Which of the following will then be true?

(a)
> If Abraham Lincoln had been born in the Aleutian Islands, he would not have been a great person.

(b)

> If Abraham Lincoln had been born in the Aleutian Islands, at least one great person would have been born there.

Why?

29. Motion cannot begin. For in order for a body to traverse a given space (or length), it must first traverse half of that length. But it cannot traverse that half unless it first traverses half of that (the quarter); and it cannot traverse the quarter unless it first traverses half of that (the eighth); and so on. Whatever distance we select, there is some other distance that must be traversed before it, and another before that, and so on. So, motion can never begin.

30. Did you know that red roses turn yellow in a totally dark room? Of course, they turn red again if they're exposed to the least bit of light.

PASSAGES

A. Plato, *Meno*

SOCRATES:	There are some who desire evil?
MENO:	Yes.
SOCRATES:	Do you mean that they think the evils which they desire to be good; or do they know that they are evil and yet desire them?
MENO:	Both, I think.
SOCRATES:	And do you really imagine, Meno, that a man knows evils to be evils and desires them notwithstanding?
MENO:	Certainly I do.
SOCRATES:	And desire is of possession?
MENO:	Yes, of possession.
SOCRATES:	And does he think that the evils will do good to him who possesses them, or does he know that they will do him harm?
MENO:	There are some who think that the evils will do them good, and others who know that they will do them harm.
SOCRATES:	And, in your opinion, do those who think that they will do them good know that they are evils?
MENO:	Certainly not.
SOCRATES:	Is it not obvious that those who are ignorant of their nature do not desire them; but they desire what they suppose to be goods although they are really evils; and if they are mistaken and suppose the evils to be goods, they really desire goods?
MENO:	Yes, in that case.
SOCRATES:	Well, and do those who, as you say, desire evils, and think that evils are hurtful to the possessor of them, know that they will be hurt by them?
MENO:	They must know it.
SOCRATES:	And must they not suppose that those who are hurt are miserable in proportion to the hurt which is inflicted upon them?

MENO:	How can it be otherwise?
SOCRATES:	But are not the miserable ill fated?
MENO:	Yes, indeed.
SOCRATES:	And does anyone desire to be miserable and ill fated?
MENO:	I should say not, Socrates.
SOCRATES:	But if there is no one who desires to be miserable, there is no one, Meno, who desires evil; for what is misery but the desire and possession of evil?
MENO:	That appears to be the truth, Socrates, and I admit that nobody desires evil.

B.   Plato, *Phaedo*

It is not at all hard to understand my meaning, Socrates replied. If, for example, the one opposite, to go to sleep, existed without the corresponding opposite, to wake up, which is generated from the first, then all nature would at last make the tale of Endymion meaningless, and he would no longer be conspicuous; for everything else would be in the same state of sleep that he was in. And if all things were compounded together and never separated, the Chaos of Anaxagoras would soon be realized. Just in the same way, my dear Cebes, if all things in which there is any life were to die, and when they were dead were to remain in that form and not come to life again, would not the necessary result be that everything at last would be dead, and nothing alive? For if living things were generated from other sources than death, and were to die, the result is inevitable that all things would be consumed by death. Is it not so?

C.   Plato, *Theaetetus*

SOCRATES:	Then what shall we say, Theaetetus, if we are asked: 'But is what you describe possible for anyone? Can any man think what is not, either about something that is or absolutely?' I suppose we must answer to that: 'Yes, when he believes something and what he believes is not true.' Or what are we to say?
THEAETETUS:	We must say that.
SOCRATES:	Then is the same sort of thing possible in any other case?
THEAETETUS:	What sort of thing?
SOCRATES:	That a man should see something, and yet what he sees should be nothing.
THEAETETUS:	No. How could that be?
SOCRATES:	Yet surely if what he sees is something, it must be a thing that is. Or do you suppose that 'something' can be reckoned among things that have no being at all?
THEAETETUS:	No, I don't.
SOCRATES:	Then, if he sees something, he sees a thing that is.
THEAETETUS:	Evidently.

SOCRATES:	And if he hears a thing, he hears something and hears a thing that is.
THEAETETUS:	Yes.
SOCRATES:	And if he touches a thing, he touches something, and if something, then a thing that is.
THEAETETUS:	That also is true.
SOCRATES:	And if he thinks, he thinks something, doesn't he?
THEAETETUS:	Necessarily.
SOCRATES:	And when he thinks something, he thinks a thing that is?
THEAETETUS:	I agree.
SOCRATES:	So to think what is not is to think nothing.
THEAETETUS:	Clearly.
SOCRATES:	But surely to think nothing is the same as not to think at all.
THEAETETUS:	That seems plain.
SOCRATES:	If so, it is impossible to think what is not, either about anything that is, or absolutely.

D. Aristotle, *Nichomachean Ethics*

Since there are evidently more than one end, and we choose some of these (e.g. wealth, flutes, and in general instruments) for the sake of something else, clearly not all ends are final ends; but the chief good is evidently something final. Therefore, if there is only one final end, this will be what we are seeking, and if there are more than one, the most final of these will be what we are seeking. Now we call that which is in itself worthy of pursuit more final than that which is worthy of pursuit for the sake of something else, and that which is never desirable for the sake of something else more final than the things that are desirable both in themselves and for the sake of that other thing, and therefore we call final without qualification that which is always desirable in itself and never for the sake of something else.

Now such a thing happiness, above all else, is held to be; for this we choose always for itself and never for the sake of something else, but honor, pleasure, reason, and every virtue we choose indeed for themselves (for if nothing resulted from them we should still choose each of them), but we choose them also for the sake of happiness, judging that by means of them we shall be happy. Happiness, on the other hand, no one chooses for the sake of these, nor, in general, for anything other than itself. . . .

Happiness, then, is something final and self-sufficient, and is [the chief good] and the end of action.

E. Augustine, *Confessions*

We speak of a long time and a short time, and we only say this of the past or future. For instance, we call a hundred years ago a long past time, and, likewise, a hundred years ahead a long future time. . . . But how is something long or short which does not exist? For, the past does not now exist and the future does not yet exist. So, let us not say: it *is* long; rather, let us say of past time: it *was* long; and of the future: it *will be* long.

. . . Was that past time long in the sense that it was long when already past, or when it was still present? Of course it could have been long only at the time when that existed which was capable of being long, but as past it was already not existing; hence, it could not be long, for it was wholly non-existent.

So let us not say past time was long; for we will discover nothing which could have been long, since, from the fact that it is past, it does not exist. Rather let us say: "That present time was long," for, when it was present, it was long. . . .

But . . . not even one day is present as a whole. It is made up of all twenty-four hours of night and day. The first of these regards the rest as future, the last one regards them as past; and the intermediate ones are to those preceding, as to the past; to those coming after, as to the future. And this one hour itself goes on by means of fleeting little parts: whatever part of it has flown by is the past; whatever remains to it is the future. If one can conceive any part of time which could not be divided into even the most minute moments, then that alone is what may be called the present, and this flies over from the future into the past so quickly that it does not extend over the slightest instant. For if it has any extension, it is divided into past and future. But the present has no length.

Where then is the time which we may call long?

F.   Anselm, *Proslogion*

And so, Lord, do thou, who dost give understanding to faith, give me, so far as thou knowest it to be profitable, to understand that thou art as we believe; and that thou art that which we believe. And, indeed, we believe that thou art a being than which nothing greater can be conceived. Or is there no such nature, since the fool hath said in his heart, there is no God? (Psalms XIV.1). But, at any rate, this very fool, when he hears of this being of which I speak—a being than which nothing greater can be conceived—understands what he hears, and what he understands is in his understanding; although he does not understand it to exist.

. . . Hence, even the fool is convinced that something exists in the understanding, at least, than which nothing greater can be conceived. For, when he hears of this, he understands it. And whatever is understood, exists in the understanding. And assuredly that, than which nothing greater can be conceived, cannot exist in the understanding alone. For, suppose it exists in the understanding alone: then it can be conceived to exist in reality; which is greater.

Therefore, if that, than which nothing greater can be conceived, exists in the understanding alone, the very being, than which nothing greater can be conceived, is one, than which a greater can be conceived. But obviously this is impossible. Hence, there is no doubt that there exists a being, than which nothing greater can be conceived, and it exists both in the understanding and in reality.

G.   Aquinas, *Summa Theologica*

The second way [to prove the existence of God] is from the nature of efficient cause. In the world of sensible things we find there is an order of efficient causes. There is no case known (neither is it, indeed, possible) in which a thing is found to be the efficient cause of itself; for so it would be prior to itself, which is impossible. Now in efficient causes it is not possible to go on to infinity, because in all efficient causes following in order, the first is the cause of the intermediate cause, and the intermediate is the cause of the ultimate cause, whether the intermediate cause be several, or one only. Now to take away the cause is to take away the effect. Therefore, if there be no first cause among efficient causes, there will be no ultimate, nor any intermediate, cause. But if in efficient causes it is possible to go on to infinity, there will be no first efficient cause, neither will there be an ultimate effect, nor any intermediate efficient causes; all of which is plainly false. Therefore it is necessary to admit a first efficient cause, to which everyone gives the name of God.

H.   Descartes, *Meditations on First Philosophy*

Nevertheless, I must remember that I am a man, and that consequently I am accustomed to sleep and in my dreams to imagine the same things that lunatics imagine when awake, or sometimes things which are even less plausible. How many times has it occurred that the quiet of the night made me dream of my usual habits: that I was here, clothed in a dressing gown, and sitting by the fire, although I was in fact lying undressed in bed! It seems apparent to me now, that I am not looking at this paper with my eyes closed, that this head that I shake is not drugged with sleep, that it is with design and deliberate intent that I stretch out this hand and perceive it. What happens in sleep seems not at all as clear and as distinct as all this. But I am speaking as though I never recall having been misled, while asleep, by similar illusions! When I consider these matters carefully, I realize so clearly that there are no conclusive indications by which waking life can be distinguished from sleep that I am quite astonished, and my bewilderment is such that it is almost able to convince me that I am sleeping.

I.1   Descartes, *Meditations on First Philosophy*

Since I know that all the things I conceive clearly and distinctly can be produced by God exactly as I conceive them, it is sufficient that I can clearly and distinctly conceive one thing apart from another to be certain that the one is distinct or different from the other. For they can be made to exist separately, at least by the omnipotence of God, and we are obliged to consider them different no matter what power produces this separation. From the very fact that I know with certainty that I exist, and that I find that absolutely nothing else belongs necessarily to my nature or essence except that I am a thinking being, I readily conclude that my essence consists solely in being a body which thinks or a substance whose whole essence or nature is only to think. And although perhaps . . . I have a body with which I am very closely united, nevertheless, since on the one hand I have a clear and distinct idea of myself in so far as I am only a thinking and not an extended being, and since on the other hand I have a distinct idea of body in so far as it is only an extended being which does not think, it is certain that this "I"— that is to say, my soul, by virtue of which I am what I am—is entirely and truly distinct from my body and that it can be or exist without it.

I.2   d'Holbach, *The System of Nature*

The beings of the human species . . . are susceptible of two sorts of motion: the one, that of the mass, by which an entire body, or some of its parts, are visibly transferred from one place to another; the other, internal and concealed, of some of which man is sensible, which so takes place without his knowledge and is not even to be guessed at, but by the effect it outwardly produces. In a machine so extremely complex as man, formed by the combination of such a multiplicity of matter, so diversified in its properties, so different in its proportions, so varied in its modes of action, the motion necessarily becomes of the most complicated kind; its dullness, as well as its rapidity, frequently escapes the observation of those themselves, in whom it takes place.

Let us not then be surprised, if when man would account to himself for his existence, for his manner of acting, finding so many obstacles to encounter,—he invented such strange hypotheses to explain the concealed spring of his machine—if when this motion appeared to him to be different from that of other bodies, he conceived an idea that he moved and acted in a manner altogether distinct from the other beings in nature. . . . He fell into the belief, that he perceived within himself a substance distinguished from that self, endowed with a secret force, in which he supposed existed qualities distinctly differing from those, of either the visible causes that acted on his organs, or those organs themselves. . . . Thus, for want of meditating nature—of considering her under her true point of view—of remarking the conformity—of noticing the simultaneity, the unity of the motion of this fancied motive-power with that of his body—of his material organs—he conjectured he was not only a distinct being, but that he was set apart, with different energies, from all the other beings in nature; that he was of a more simple essence, having nothing in common with any thing by which he was surrounded; nothing that connected him with all that he beheld.

It is from thence has successively sprung his notions of *spirituality, immateriality, immortality;* in short, all those vague unmeaning words, he has invented by degrees, in order to subtilize and designate the attributes of the unknown power, which he believes he contains within himself. . . .

J. Locke, *An Essay Concerning Human Understanding*

This may show us wherein personal identity consists: not in the identity of substance, but, as I have said, in the identity of consciousness, wherein if Socrates and the present mayor of Queinborough agree, they are the same person: if the same Socrates waking and sleeping do not partake of the same consciousness, Socrates waking and sleeping is not the same person. And to punish Socrates waking for what sleeping Socrates thought, and waking Socrates was never conscious of, would be no more of right, than to punish one twin for what his brother-twin did, whereof he knew nothing, because their outsides were so like, that they could not be distinguished; for such twins have been seen.

K. Locke, *An Essay Concerning Human Understanding*

Words, by long and familiar use, . . . come to excite in men certain ideas so constantly and readily, that they are apt to suppose a natural connexion between them. But that they signify only men's peculiar ideas, and that *by a perfect arbitrary imposition,* is evident, in that they often fail to excite in others (even that use the same language) the same ideas we take them to be signs of: and every man has so inviolable a liberty to make words stand for what ideas he pleases, that no one hath the power to make others have the same ideas in their minds that he has, when they use the same words that he does. . . . It is true, common use, by a tacit consent, appropriates certain sounds to certain ideas in all languages, which so far limits the signification of that sound, that unless a man applies it to the same idea, he does not speak properly: . . . But whatever be the consequence of any man's using of words differently, either from their general meaning, or the particular sense of the person to whom he addresses them; this is certain, their signification, in his use of them, is limited to his ideas, and they can be signs of nothing else.

L.1   Hume, *A Treatise of Human Nature*

For my part, when I enter most intimately into what I call *myself,* I always stumble on some particular perception or other, of heat or cold, light or shade, love or hatred, pain or pleasure. I never can catch *myself* at any time without a perception, and never can observe any thing but the perception. When my perceptions are removed for any time, as by sound sleep, so long am I insensible of *myself,* and may truly be said not to exist. And were all my perceptions removed by death, and could I neither think, nor feel, nor see, nor love, nor hate after the dissolution of my body, I should be entirely annihilated, nor do I conceive what is farther requisite to make me a perfect nonentity. If any one upon serious and unprejudiced reflexion, thinks he has a different notion of *himself,* I must confess I can reason no longer with him. . . . He may, perhaps, perceive something simple and continued, which he calls *himself;* tho' I am certain there is no such principle in me.

But setting aside some metaphysicians of this kind, I may venture to affirm of the rest of mankind, that they are nothing but a bundle of collection of different perceptions, which succeed each other with an inconceivable rapidity, and are in a perpetual flux and movement. . . . The mind is a kind of theatre, where several perceptions successively make their appearances; pass, re-pass, glide away, and mingle in an infinite variety of postures and situations. There is properly no *simplicity* in it at one time, nor *identity* in different; whatever natural propension we may have to imagine that simplicity and identity. The comparison of the theatre must not mislead us. They are the successive perceptions only, that constitute the mind; nor have we the most distant notion of the place, where these scenes are represented, or of the materials, of which it is composed.

L.2   Reid, *Essays on the Intellectual Powers of Man*

My personal identity . . . implies the continued existence of that indivisible thing which I call *myself.* Whatever this self may be, it is something which thinks, and deliberates, and resolves, and acts, and suffers. My thoughts, and actions, and feelings, change every moment; they have no continued, but a successive, existence; but that *self,* or *I,* to which they belong, is permanent, and has the same relation to all the succeeding thoughts, actions, and feelings which I call mine. . . .

The proper evidence I have of all this is *remembrance.* I remember that twenty years ago I conversed with such a person; I remember several things that passed in that conversation: my memory testifies, not only that this was done, but that it was done by me who now remembers it. If it was done by me, I must have existed at that time, and continued to exist from that time to the present: if the identical person whom I call myself had not a part in that conversation, my memory is fallacious; it gives a distinct and positive testimony of what is not true. Every man in his senses believes what he distinctly remembers, and everything he remembers convinces him that he existed at the time remembered.

M.1   Locke, letter to the Bishop of Worcester

"Everything that has a beginning must have a cause" is a true principle of reason or a proposition certainly true; which we come to know by . . . contemplating our ideas and perceiving that the idea of beginning to be is necessarily connected with the idea of some operation; and the idea of operation with the idea of something operating which we call a cause. And so the beginning to be is perceived to agree with the idea of a cause, as is expressed in the proposition, and thus it comes to be a certain proposition, and so may be called a principle of reason, as every true proposition is to him that perceives the certainty of it.

M.2   Hume, *A Treatise of Human Nature*

'Tis a general maxim in philosophy, that *whatever begins to exist, must have a cause of existence*. This is commonly taken for granted in all reasonings, without any proof given or demanded. . . .

But here is an argument, which proves at once, that the foregoing proposition is neither intuitively nor demonstrably certain. We can never demonstrate the necessity of a cause to every new existence, or new modification of existence, without showing at the same time the impossibility there is, that any thing can ever begin to exist without some productive principle; and where the latter proposition cannot be proved, we must despair of ever being able to prove the former. Now that the latter proposition is utterly incapable of a demonstrative proof, we may satisfy ourselves by considering, that as all distinct ideas are separable from each other, and as the ideas of cause and effect are evidently distinct, 'twill be easy for us to conceive any object to be nonexistent this moment, and existent the next, without conjoining to it the distinct idea of a cause or productive principle. The separation, therefore, of the idea of a cause from that of a beginning of existence, is plainly possible for the imagination; and consequently the actual separation of these objects is so far possible, that it implies no contradiction nor absurdity; and is therefore incapable of being refuted by any reasoning from mere ideas; without which 'tis impossible to demonstrate the necessity of a cause.

Accordingly we shall find upon examination, that every demonstration, which has been produced for the necessity of a cause, is fallacious and sophistical.

N.　Mill, *Utilitarianism*

The only proof capable of being given that an object is visible, is that people actually see it; the only proof that a sound is audible, is that people hear it: and so of the other sources of our experience. In like manner, I apprehend, the sole evidence it is possible to produce that any thing is desirable, is that people do actually desire it. If the end which the utilitarian doctrine proposes to itself were not, in theory and in practice, acknowledged to be an end, nothing could ever convince any person that it was so. No reason can be given why the general happiness is desirable, except that each person, so far as he believes it to be attainable, desires his own phappiness. This, however, being a fact, we have not only all the proof which the case admits of, but all which it is possible to require, that happiness is a good; that each person's happiness is a good to that person; and the general happiness, therefore, a good to the aggregate of all persons. Happiness has made out its title as *one* of the ends of conduct, and consequently one of the criteria of morality.

O.　Russell, *The Problems of Philosophy*

It is sometimes said that 'light *is* a form of wave-motion,' but this is misleading, for the light which we immediately see, which we know directly by means of our senses, is *not* a form of wave-motion, but something quite different—something which we all know if we are not blind, though we cannot describe it so as to convey our knowledge to a man who is blind. A wave-motion, on the contrary, could quite well be described to a blind man, since he can acquire a knowledge of space by the sense of touch; and he can experience a wave-motion by a sea voyage almost as well as we can. But this, which a blind man can understand, is not what we mean by *light:* we mean by *light* just that which a blind man can never understand, and which we can never describe to him.

P.　Russell, *The Problems of Philosophy*

Consider such a proposition as 'Edinburgh is north of London.' Here we have a relation between two places, and it seems plain that the relation subsists independently of our knowledge of it. When we come to know that Edinburgh is north of London, we come to know something which has only to do with Edinburgh and London: we do not cause the truth of the proposition by coming to know it, on the contrary we merely apprehend a fact which was there before we knew it. The part of the earth's surface where Edinburgh stands would be north of the part where London stands, even if there were no human beings to know about north and south, and even if there were no minds at all in the universe. . . .

This conclusion, however, is met by the difficulty that the relation 'north of' does not seem to *exist* in the same sense in which Edinburgh and London exist. If we ask 'Where and when does this relation exist?' the answer must be 'Nowhere and nowhen'. There is no place or time where we can find the relation 'north of'. It does not exist in Edinburgh any more than in London, for it relates the two and is neutral as between them. Nor can we say that it exists at any particular time. Now everything that can be apprehended by the senses or by introspection exists at some particular time. Hence the relation 'north of' is radically different from such things. It is neither in space nor in time, neither material nor mental; yet it is something.

Q.   C. S. Lewis, *Miracles*

We may in fact state it as a rule that *no thought is valid if it can be fully explained as the result of irrational causes*. Every reader of this book applies this rule automatically all day long. When a sober man tells you that the house is full of rats or snakes, you attend to him: if you know that his belief in the rats and snakes is due to *delirium tremens* you do not even bother to look for them. If you even *suspect* an irrational cause, you begin to pay less attention to a man's beliefs; your friend's pessimistic view of the European situation alarms you less when you discover that he is suffering from a bad liver attack. Conversely, when we discover a belief to be false we then first look about for irrational causes ("I was tired"—"I was in a hurry"—"I wanted to believe it"). . . . All thoughts which are so caused are valueless. We never, in our ordinary thinking, admit any exceptions to this rule.

Now it would clearly be preposterous to apply this rule to each particular thought as we come to it and yet not to apply it to all thoughts taken collectively, that is, to human reason as a whole. Each particular thought is valueless if it is the result of irrational causes. Obviously, then, the whole process of human thought, what we call Reason, is equally valueless if it is the result of irrational causes. Hence every theory of the universe which makes the human mind a result of irrational causes is inadmissible, for it would be a proof that there are no such things as proofs. Which is nonsense.

But Naturalism, as commonly held, is precisely a theory of this sort. The mind, like every other particular thing or event, is supposed to be simply the product of the Total System. It is supposed to be that and nothing more, to have no power whatever of "going on its own accord." And the Total System is not supposed to be rational. All thoughts whatever are therefore the results of irrational causes, and nothing more than that.

R.1   Moore, *Principia Ethica*

In fact, if it is not the case that 'good' denotes something simple and indefinable, only two alternatives are possible: either it is a complex, a given whole, about the correct analysis of which there may be disagreement; or else it means nothing at all. . . .

The hypothesis that disagreement about the meaning of good is disagreement with regard to the correct analysis of a given whole, may be most plainly seen to be incorrect by consideration of the fact that, whatever definition be offered, it may be always asked, with significance, of the complex so defined, whether it is itself good. To take, for instance, one of the more plausible, because one of the more complicated, of such proposed definitions, it may easily be thought, at first sight, that to be good may mean to be that which we desire to desire. Thus if we apply this definition to a particular instance and say 'When we think that A is good, we are thinking that A is one of the things which we desire to desire,' our proposition may seem quite plausible. But, if we carry the investigation further, and ask ourselves 'Is it good to desire to desire A?' it is apparent, on a little reflection, that this question is itself as intelligible, as the original question 'Is A good?'—that we are, in fact, now asking for exactly the same information about the desire to desire A, for which we formerly asked with regard to A itself. . . .

And the same consideration is sufficient to dismiss the hypothesis that 'good' has no meaning whatsoever. . . . Whoever will attentively consider with himself what is actually before his mind when he asks the question 'Is pleasure (or whatever it may be) after all good?' can easily satisfy himself that he is not merely wondering whether pleasure is pleasant. . . . Everyone does in fact understand the question 'Is this good?' When he thinks of it, his state of mind is different from what it would be, were he asked 'Is this pleasant, or desired, or approved?' It has a distinct meaning for him, even though he may not recognize in what respect it is distinct. . . .

'Good,' then, is indefinable.

R.2   Ayer, *Language, Truth, and Logic*

We begin by admitting that the fundamental ethical concepts are unanalysable, inasmuch as there is no criterion by which one can test the validity of the judgements in which they occur. So far we are in agreement with the absolutists. But, unlike the absolutists, we are able to give an explanation of this fact about ethical concepts. We say that the reason why they are unanalysable is that they are mere pseudo-concepts. The presence of an ethical symbol in a proposition adds nothing to its factual content. Thus if I say to someone, "You acted wrongly in stealing that money," I am not stating anything more than if I had simply said, "You stole that money." In adding that this action is wrong I am not making any further statement about it. I am simply evincing my moral disapproval of it. It is as if I had said, "You stole that money," in a peculiar tone of horror, or written it with the addition of some special exclamation marks. The tone, or the exclamation marks, adds nothing to the literal meaning of the sentence. It merely serves to show that the expression of it is attended by certain feelings in the speaker.

S.1 Ayer, *The Problem of Knowledge*

For example, I am now seated in a vineyard: and I can fairly claim to know that there are clusters of grapes a few feet away from me. But in making even such a simple statement as 'that is a bunch of grapes,' a statement so obvious that in ordinary conversation, as opposed, say, to an English lesson, it would never be made, I am in a manner going beyond my evidence. I can see the grapes: but it is requisite also that in the appropriate conditions I should be able to touch them. They are not real grapes if they are not tangible; and from the fact that I am having just these visual experiences, it would seem that nothing logically follows about what I can or cannot touch. Neither is it enough that I can see and touch the grapes: other people must be able to perceive them too. If I had reason to believe that no one else could, in the appropriate conditions, see or touch them, I should be justified in concluding that I was undergoing a hallucination. Thus, while my basis for making this assertion may be very strong, so strong indeed as to warrant a claim to knowledge, it is not conclusive; my experience, according to this argument, could still be what it is even though the grapes which I think that I am perceiving really do not exist.

S.2 Austin, *Sense and Sensibilia*

If I watch for some time an animal a few feet in front of me, in a good light, if I prod it perhaps, sniff, and take note of the noises it makes, I may say, 'That's a pig'; and this too will be 'incorrigible,' nothing could be produced that would show that I had made a mistake. . . .

The situation in which I would properly be said to have *evidence* for the statement that some animal is a pig is that, for example, in which the beast itself is not actually on view, but I can see plenty of pig-like marks on the ground outside its retreat. If I find a few buckets of pig-food, that's a bit more evidence, and the noises and the smell may provide better evidence still. But if the animal then emerges and stands there plainly in view, but there is no longer any question of collecting evidence; its coming into view doesn't provide me with more *evidence* that it's a pig, I can now just *see* that it is, the question is settled.

NOTES
TO THE PASSAGES

A. Plato, *Meno,* in *The Dialogues of Plato* trans. Benjamin Jowett, 4th ed. 1953 (Oxford University Press).

B. Plato, *Phaedo,* trans. F. J. Church (Indianapolis and New York: Bobbs-Merrill, 1951), p. 19.

C. Plato, *Theaetetus,* in Francis M. Cornford, *Plato's Theory of Knowledge* (New Jersey: Humanities Press Inc., 1957), pp. 114–15.

D. Aristotle, *Nichomachean Ethics* (1097a, b), in Richard McKeon, *The Basic Works of Aristotle* (New York: Random House, 1941), pp. 941–42.

E. Augustine, *Confessions* (Bk. 11, Chap. 14–15), trans. Vernon J. Bourke, Fathers of the Church Series, Vol. 5 (Washington, D.C.: Catholic University of America Press, 1953), pp. 343–46.

F. Anselm, *Proslogion* (Chap. II), trans. S. N. Deane. Reprinted by permission of The Open Court Publishing Company (1961 edition; introduction by Charles Hartshorne), LaSalle, Illinois.

G. Thomas Aquinas, *Summa Theologica* (Part I, Q2, Art 3), in A. C. Pegis, *Introduction to St. Thomas Aquinas* (New York: Random House, 1948), pp. 25–26.

H. René Descartes, *Meditations on First Philosophy,* trans. Laurence J. Lafleur (Indianapolis and New York: Bobbs-Merrill, 1960), pp. 18–19.

I.1 Descartes, *Meditations,* pp. 73–74.

I.2 Baron Paul d'Holbach, *The System of Nature,* trans. H. D. Robinson (New York: Burt Franklin, 1970), Chap. VI.

J. John Locke, *An Essay Concerning Human Understanding,* Vol. 1 (II, xxvii, 1g), (New York: Dover, 1959), p. 460.

K. Locke, *Essay,* Vol. 2 (III, ii, 8), p. 12.

L.1 David Hume, *A Treatise of Human Nature* (I, iv, 6), ed. L. A. Selby-Bigge (London: Oxford University Press, 1888), pp. 252–53.

L.2 Thomas Reid, *Essays on the Intellectual Powers of Man* (III, 4), ed. A. D. Woozley (London: Macmillan, 1941), p. 203.

M.1 John Locke, letter to the Right Rev. Edward Lord Bishop of Worcester, in *Works* Vol. 4 (London, 1812), pp. 61–62.

M.2 Hume, *Treatise* (I, iii, 3), pp. 78–80.

N. John Stuart Mill, *Utilitarianism,* in Marshall Cohen, *The Philosophy of John Stuart Mill* (New York: Random House, 1961), p. 363.

O. Bertrand Russell, *The Problems of Philosophy* (New York: Oxford University Press, 1959), p. 28.

P. Russell, *The Problems of Philosophy,* pp. 97–98.

Q. C. S. Lewis, *Miracles* (New York: Macmillan, 1947), pp. 20–22.

R.1 G. E. Moore, *Principia Ethica* (London: Cambridge University Press, 1903), pp. 15–17.

R.2 A. J. Ayer, *Language, Truth, and Logic* (New York: Dover, 1952), p. 107.

S.1 A. J. Ayer, *The Problem of Knowledge* (Baltimore: Penguin, 1956), pp. 56–57.

S.2 J. L. Austin, *Sense and Sensibilia* (London: Oxford University Press, 1962), pp. 114–15.